THE MISSION
DRIVEN PARISH

THE MISSION DRIVEN PARISH

PATRICK J. BRENNAN

ORBIS BOOKS
Maryknoll, New York 10545

Founded in 1970, Orbis Books endeavors to publish works that enlighten the mind, nourish the spirit, and challenge the conscience. The publishing arm of the Maryknoll Fathers and Brothers, Orbis seeks to explore the global dimensions of the Christian faith and mission, to invite dialogue with diverse cultures and religious traditions, and to serve the cause of reconciliation and peace. The books published reflect the views of their authors and do not represent the official position of the Maryknoll Society. To learn more about Maryknoll and Orbis Books, please visit our website at www.maryknoll.com.

Library of Congress Cataloging-in-Publication Data

Brennan, Patrick J.
    The mission driven parish / Patrick J. Brennan.
      p. cm.
    Includes index.
    ISBN 978-1-57075-692-4 (pbk.)
    1. Church. 2. Catholic Church – Doctrines. 3. Mission of the church.
4. Parishes. I. Title.
BX1746.B73 2007
262 – dc22

                                           2006034278

To the people of Holy Family Parish

Thank you for wonderfully rich years,
co-laboring for the Reign of God

Contents

Preface

I N THEIR MASTERFUL WORK *Constants in Context: A Theology of Mission for Today,* Stephen B. Bevans and Roger P. Schroeder build on the seminal work of Andrew Walls in articulating six constants that are always present in the mission activity of the church:

1. Christology, or the proclamation of Jesus and the Reign of God

2. Ecclesiology, a living theology of church

3. Eschatology, an orientation toward the future and the end of time

4. Salvation, helping the world to achieve the integrity God wills for the world

5. Anthropology, a vision of what it means to be human

6. Culture, a sensitivity to the culture in which the work is being done

The authors go on to discuss activities and characteristics of mission. In 1981, SEDOS, an organization of men's and women's religious congregations, named four principal activities of mission work:

1. Proclamation of Jesus and the Reign of God

2. Dialogue with people

3. Inculturation, planting the seed of the gospel in a local culture

4. Liberation of the poor

The five characteristics of mission according to the Vatican Secretariat for Non-Christians (1984) are:

1. Presence and witness

2. Commitment to social development and human liberation

3. Liturgical life

4. Prayer and contemplation

5. Inter-religious dialogue

6. Proclamation and catechesis

Bevans and Schroeder mention three strains of mission theology in the last quarter of the twentieth century:

1. Mission as participation in the life and mission of the Trinity

2. Mission as continuation of the mission of Jesus, to preach, serve, and witness to the justice of God's already, but not yet, Reign

3. Mission as the proclamation of Christ as the world's only Savior

The authors call for a renewed approach to mission in the twenty-first century, and they call that approach prophetic dialogue. The dialogue needed for the future of mission work, they say, is with the poor, with culture, and with other religions. Such a dialogical approach to mission must be prophetic in that it needs to share the life of the poor and to speak out against what keeps them poor. It needs to appreciate and critique human culture and guard against any leveling of cultural differences. Such dialogue needs to engage in the truth of other religions, while maintaining the conviction that Jesus is the way, the truth, and the life.

Whenever mission work is done, but certainly in the twenty-first century, the people in mission work always need to be aware of the following contexts in which the work is accomplished:

1. The socio-political context

2. The religious context, or what is happening on the stage of world religions

3. The institutional context, or what is going on in the organizations that structure and govern mission around the world

It is my hope that some of the rich theological principles of Bevans and Schroeder's book have been successfully popularized and enfleshed in the pastoral ideas I share in this book.

I want to thank many people who contributed to the writing of this book, especially the people and staff of Holy Family Parish. I wish to offer a special thank you to Paula Nowicki, who collaborated with me in putting together the manuscript.

Chapter One

Living the Reign of God

I N THE EARLY 1990s, Gerald A. Arbuckle wrote a book entitled
Refounding the Church. He spoke of the church as an organism
forever in need of renewal and adaptation for different times and
environments. With prophetic intuition, he warned against another
force that he felt emerging in our church. Arbuckle lamented that
many in leadership in the church, rather than being about the work
of refounding, were more about restorationism, which he described
as an attempt to debunk the vision and practice of Vatican II and
return to a vision and practice of the church that existed before the
Second Vatican Council.

Unfortunately, Arbuckle could not have been more on target.
Those of us who grew up during, and were transformed by, Vatican II, and who invested in the vision and pastoral practices of the
council, are now looked upon as liberals, left-wingers, or dissidents.
I personally was banned from speaking in the Archdiocese of Boston
in the 1990s.

In this culture of restorationism, creative pastors and pastoral ministers strive to "fly under the radar." They attempt to keep their
creativity and pastoral sensitivity alive by investing in their people.

Lay supporters of such restorationist approaches take photo-
graphs, carry tape recorders, and make notes on pastors, priests, and
pastoral ministers who they believe are "breaking the laws." When
downtown officials receive accusations against such pastoral leaders,
the pastoral leaders are often called in for correction or punishment.

Indeed there are models of excellence in parish evangelization and
parish ministry, but the staffs that empower and animate such models
are generally ignored by church leadership. If not ignored, they sometimes are almost made to feel guilty for thinking and doing "out of

the box." In dioceses where there are models of excellence in parish life, those models ought to be held up. Pastors and staffs ought to be encouraged to stay on in their roles in ministries. Research from Protestant churches indicates that successful Protestant churches attribute a great deal of their success to pastors with long terms.

The partnering of parishes, or the sister parish concept, which is prevalent in dioceses, should not just be one of sharing material resources. Parishes ought to help one another become models of excellence in evangelization and parish ministry. When closed-minded, judgmental ideologies prevail in diocesan or pastoral settings, the creative, life-giving mentoring that is needed to aid parishes in their evangelistic responsibilities is not present.

Near Holy Family, where I serve, is a large evangelical church, Willow Creek Community Church. The church has spawned a movement called the Willow Creek Association. In this association, member churches learn from the primary church, Willow Creek, and brother and sister churches throughout the metropolitan area, the country, and now the world. We need such teaching, mentoring alliances in the Catholic Church. I spoke of this need years ago in a previous book, *Parishes That Excel*.

Whenever church leaders, or any of us in pastoral ministry, use power on each other to advance our ideological stands, we are abusing one another, and ultimately the Body of Christ, the church.

Paralysis

Christian sociologist Tony Campolo in his book *Speaking My Mind* analyzes why evangelical churches are outstripping mainline denominational churches in terms of popularity, attendance, and evangelical effectiveness. He sees the traditional Protestant and Catholic churches as "frozen" in methodology and organization, while the younger evangelical churches are often blessed with entrepreneurial pastors whose worship services inculturate the gospel message for a people who have grown up with and are surrounded by media, technology, and entertainment. In referencing Campolo, I am not saying that I agree with or support all that evangelical churches do, but his comment on organizational frozenness is right on target with regard to too many Catholic parishes.

In this culture of restorationism, people seem afraid to think, to ask questions, to seriously discuss the future direction of the church. Indeed, many hard questions are going to have to be discussed if Catholic parishes are going to avoid massive membership erosion, lack of resources, and closings. Often parishes that close have enormous populations of multi-cultural people within them. Church leaders and pastoral leaders have not engaged in the creative conversations and planning that are required for the effective evangelization of people of multi-generations and cultures.

Such conversations and planning cannot happen if certain issues regarding present and future pastoral life are just taken off the table and are not allowed to be talked about. Silence about issues that need to be talked about — in our personal lives, our relationships, and church life — can be a sign of a lack of health and wholeness.

What is needed for the future of parish life is radical commitment to the Reign of God, without paralyzing ideological control, or the bashing or banishing of one another. What is at stake is the good of the church and future parish life. If our real concerns are people, their salvation, the emergence of the Reign of God, and the health of the Body of Christ, the church, then all of us in positions of leadership must commit ourselves to humble listening, communication, discernment, and conflict resolution. Future effectiveness in pastoral ministry is not in victory by either liberal or conservative ideologies, but rather in our common pursuit of God's truth and organically grown strategies that propagate the gospel message and God's Reign in the cultures that we live in. Stephen Bevans and Roger Schroeder in *Constants in Context* say that the vision and methodology for mission work in the future needs to be prophetic dialogue, many strata of people in prayerful dialogue about God's truth.

On the first Holy Thursday night, Jesus washed feet. He modeled servant leadership. He told his disciples and us to do the same. The priesthood emerged first in Jewish communities converting to

Christianity; the episcopacy was born in Hellenistic communities converting to Christianity. In the first century, the boundaries separating
presbyters and bishops were often not clear. Eventually, ordination
to the roles of deacon, presbyter, and *episcopos* evolved. But Jesus
did not set up ordained ministry the way we know it today. It has
been shaped and fashioned by human minds and hands, and it could
be shaped and fashioned anew if church leaders could break out of
ideological paralysis and show enough love for the church to make
necessary changes to ensure that there are priests and bishops and
deacons in the future.

Tom Rainer, writing in *Church Executive* magazine, predicts that
tens of thousands of mainline churches will close by the year 2010.
They are churches populated by the group he calls "the loyalists,"
who were born before 1946. Loyalists, he says, supported churches
whether services and homilies were effective or not. That generation is
aging, and the generations that have followed the loyalists, those born
after 1946, do not have the same blind dedication. More deliberate
efforts at evangelizing are needed for those born between 1946 and our
own day, if parishes and congregations are going to survive and grow.

In the last several years we have witnessed the illness of the institutional church becoming apparent. The first level of this revelation
of pathology was in the public's growing awareness of the sexual
abuse of minors by priests. Not only did this expose the abuse of
children; it exposed how abusive the whole institutional hierarchical
system can be. Not only were the abused abused; the abusers were
victims of abuse. They were trained and formed in seminary systems
that denied and repressed the reality of human sexuality. Anything
human that is repressed can become distorted and may reappear in
some distorted fashion. Thus it is with human sexuality and ordained
priests. Some are psychosexually stunted, psychosexually about the
same age as the young people they abused. While personality traits,
genetic factors, and family backgrounds all may have contributed toward the personality types of abusers, the seminary was the soil and
toxic nurturance that was given to these personality types.

The cover-ups of the sexual crimes, moving abusers around, and
settling with victims' families financially became almost as horrific as

the acts of abuse. The financial settlements, which bankrupted some dioceses, became a source of scandal. People became uncertain about where their money was going and for what it was being used. Many who supported the church and their parishes financially for decades began to withdraw funds or donate funds to other needy causes rather than supporting the church.

In the midst of all this darkness, some people have strayed from the church and their parishes, often with cynicism. Others have dropped away from church attendance and involvement, becoming bored, apathetic, and cynical about church-related matters. Other Catholics have gone to other denominations, chiefly evangelical churches. While we might look at the theology of some of these churches as lacking in substance, their congregations are warm, welcoming, spirited, with heartfelt worship, opportunities for small Christian communities, and opportunities for many kinds of involvement, either serving others or being served in some area of need.

This phenomenon does not seem to bother some bishops. I have heard comments from some that effectively have said, "If people can't conform to what it means to be Catholic, let them go to other churches that suit them better."

To rub salt into many Catholics' wounds, Cardinal Bernard Law, rather than being challenged and punished for his irresponsible behavior, was rewarded with a well-paying administrative job in the Vatican. Like most addictive people and organizations, the church hides behind a pretense of perfection: "Everything is just fine with us."

Servant Leadership for the Reign of God

In the face of what I have described thus far, it is absolutely vital that Catholic laity discover what Stephen Covey calls their "voice" in his book *The 8th Habit*. I was told recently of a conference at which a bishop spoke. His tone was authoritarian and demeaning. While some of the people in attendance walked out on the bishop, most of them sat there silent, hurt, angry, and feeling infantilized. Church leadership still has a controlling power over many of us.

I am sure they do not intend it, but many of our church leaders are destroying the church. If the church is to be saved, it must be saved by concerned laity who stand up and give voice to the *sensus fidelium,* the sense of the faithful. The truth, the Holy Spirit, is at work not just in bishops, but also in the entire people of God. That voice can take various forms and shapes. It may involve how people share their resources. It may involve a demand for dialogue. It may involve study together of church history, a study that would liberate us from constraining ideological stands and help us refound and re-shape the church for the future. Catholic laity must find their voice to save the church.

What is sorely absent in the kind of church that we are part of today is a spirit of servant leadership among the hierarchy and pastors of the church. Servant leaders lead by serving. What we have too much of is authoritarianism rather than people of true authority. Rather than leaders pursuing truth and the will of God, we have ideologues. We are lacking in visionary leaders, leaders who have taken the time to discern and articulate what they believe to have been the mission and vision of Jesus.

What has suffered the most at the hands of the ideologues and their ideologies? They give hardly any attention to what Jesus was most about. The very first words out of Jesus' mouth in Mark, a literary tip-off that this might be important, are these: "I have good news for you. The Reign of God is here. Change your lives." In Luke 4:43, a parallel passage, Jesus says: "Let us move to the other towns, that I might proclaim the Reign of God there also, for that is why I came."

Donald Senior and Carroll Stuhlmueller in their classic *Biblical Foundations of Mission* say that the latter passage is especially clear about Jesus' intention. He saw the Reign of God to be his mission. If it was *his* mission, it certainly ought to be the mission of his followers. The church has been preaching and teaching the church, and not enough the Reign of God. The church is, at best, a servant of the more important and greater reality, the Reign of God.

Theologians and scripture scholars have written intellectual volumes on what Jesus meant by the Reign of God. I would like to share a few of my own thoughts that are more personal in nature.

For me, what Jesus meant by the Reign of God is all tied up in his understanding of God as *Abba,* "my own dear Father, Dada, Papa." A pious Jew of Jesus' age might have been shocked at the closeness and intimacy Jesus had with his Creator/Parent.

Hans Küng, Elizabeth Johnson, Thomas Groome, and others who have given the Reign of God serious thought believe that his experience of *Abba* is foundational to what he meant by God's Reign.

Living the Reign of God is to live a God-centered life, in close, intentional relationship with *Abba.*

Life in the Reign of God is a life of prayerfulness, a prayerfulness that connected Jesus, and can connect us, with presence, grace, and Spirit in this inner environment of oneness with God.

Life in the Reign of God is not a reactive life. It strives to discern God's will in all situations.

Life in God's Reign is a non-violent, non-aggressive life.

Life in God's Reign is characterized by unconditional love of all people, service, servant leadership, stewardship of one's resources, mercy, and justice.

Life in God's Reign is about mediating God's healing power to and with each other.

Life in God's Reign is a lifelong journey of repentance, conversion, and inner transformation.

Life in God's Reign is the experience of communion with our fellow human beings.

Life in God's Reign is paschal, that is, defined by passage. People in the Reign of God are awakened to the mystery of life, death, and resurrection going on throughout their lifetimes. Life, through death, to resurrection is the core process of all of life.

Life in God's Reign is *ultimately* paschal in the sense that God invites us, through the mystery of physical death, into a new dimension of being that we call eternal life.

Much more could be said, and I will try to further develop what Jesus meant by the Reign of God throughout the book, but this is the mission that the church must be about. If we were serious about talking about, praying about, studying and conversing about God's Reign, we would be dwelling always on the ultimate meaning of life that Jesus has communicated to us through his teaching, parables, and miracles.

Martin Seligman and others were quoted in a January 17, 2005, *Time* magazine cover story entitled "The Science of Happiness." Seligman highlighted three ingredients in people's experience of genuine happiness: pleasure, engagement with others (marriage, friendship, work, hobbies), and the discovery of meaning in life. Seligman says his research has led him to see that the least important of the three is pleasure, and that which brings greatest happiness to people's lives is engagement with others and the discovery of meaning. We live in a culture that promotes the first: pursue and find pleasure, and then you will be happy. Life in God's Reign promotes the latter two: engagement with each other and discovery of meaning.

Life in God's Reign is not a call to live a painful life. It is the nature of being human to have to suffer and experience pain at different times throughout a lifetime. I have come to believe, however, that whenever individuals or communities begin to take God's Reign seriously, other forces emerge with the intention of "crucifying" Reign of God people. Their truth and non-aggression become very attractive to many people, thus threatening ideologues and their ideologies.

Life in God's Reign is an attempt to be happy, to be well, to be whole, to be holy. This was the mission of Jesus. If we are to be true to him, hierarchy, clergy, religious, and laity must take *his* mission more seriously. Let there be an end to the promotion of restorationist ideology and more of a commitment to understanding and helping with the emergence of the Reign of God. If we do this, there is a chance that decaying Catholicism might survive.

Chapter Two

The Parish as Tool
for Wholeness and Health

W HY WOULD ANYONE come to a Catholic parish, or a Christian congregation, in this technological, post-religious age of secularity? Adult learning theory has told us for years that adults are very practical people. They come to events, they come to places that help them to live and to satisfy basic human needs. Being part of a faith community ought to offer the reward, or payoff, of somehow making life better. I do not think that "better" is necessarily an emotional high from manipulative, high-spirited services or worship. Worship is, indeed, an aid if it is done well, but there are deeper realities that I think people are in need of, and need from parishes, if parishes are going to be effective in the future.

The Pursuit of Happiness

One of the deep realities of life that people are seeking is happiness. Jesus says, in the Gospel of John 15:11, "I have told you this so that my joy might be in you and your joy might be complete." It seems, according to Jesus, it is God's will for us that we be happy.

A parish ought to help people discover joy and happiness. One of the people quoted in the *Time* magazine study mentioned above is a psychologist from the University of Illinois named Edward Diener. Diener found in his research that material possessions did not bring an increase of happiness to people's lives. People seem to have a threshold for the need for material resources. If that threshold is met, or those basic needs are satisfied, accumulating more material resources does not seem to alter the happiness quotient.

Diener discovered that happiness is found in people in long-lasting, solid marriages. He found happiness in people with strong friendships and in people who had a life-influencing faith and spirituality. His recommendation is that people pursuing happiness ought to place themselves in situations in which relational skills and basic spirituality skills can be developed.

Another person working in the area of happiness is California psychologist Sonja Lyubomirsky. She has discovered that happiness is found in people who deliberately attend to their blessings on a regular basis, even journaling those blessings. She found happiness in people who do random acts of kindness for each other. People who take the time to savor life's joys discover what happiness is. People who learn to forgive grow in happiness. People who express gratitude to others for the contributions those others make in their lives can be happy people. She also emphasizes the importance of investing in family and friends. She adds two other components to happiness: working on a program of health and wellness and learning stress management skills.

Michael McCullough, associate professor of psychology and religious studies at the University of Miami, has found a strong correlation between faith and happiness. McCullough and his associates have found that the disciplines of faith (prayer, worship, devotion, ministry) and the relationships that come with faith (small communities, the community at worship) contribute significantly both to the relief of depression and to happiness.

McCullough suggests that the people of faith he has studied have a remarkable resiliency in the face of struggle, disappointment, sickness, and loss, the experiences that we sometimes categorize under the theological image of the cross. Faith and spirituality give people courage to face life's mysteries and struggles.

Seeking Communion

Besides happiness, McCullough and others highlight another basic human need related to happiness that parishes and congregations can help people with. I think the Creation accounts in the book of Genesis say, at root, that human beings have been made for communion, union, with, connection. We have been made for communion with God, and we have been made for communion with one another, in many different ways, on many different levels. Parishes ought to be places and opportunities where we do not experience more of American isolation, independence, and competition. They ought to be places where we enter into genuine communion, with God and each other.

Scott Peck lamented years ago that most parishes and congregations in the United States offer what he called pseudo-community rather than genuine community. Bernard Lee and Michael Cowan, in their book *Dangerous Memories,* outline for us the ingredients of true spiritual community, whether that is experienced on a large scale or in a small group. Those ingredients are prayer and worship; an encounter with the scriptural word; koinonia, or the sharing of life with one another; and service to one's community, the larger faith community, and the world around us. Parishes and congregations ought to be offering people experiences of such genuine community.

Just looking at the happiness research and the theological, psychological, and sociological research being done on community, a parish committed to excellence has many indicators of what its work ought to be like in the future. Here I want to mention briefly some of the programs we have developed at Holy Family Parish. We will consider these in more detail in the chapters that follow.

At Holy Family Parish we have over fifteen hundred people in Small Christian Communities, Bible Study groups, Awareness groups, and Focus groups. Most of the Small Christian Communities are lectionary-based, focused on the readings for the following Sunday. The Bible Study groups focus on different books or themes from sacred scripture. The Awareness groups focus on books or movies. Their intention is to help people grow in awareness of spiritual and justice-related issues that will lead them to action. These groups retain some time for lectionary-based faith sharing. Focus groups have emerged from some shared experience like Marriage Encounter or a retreat model that we call Kingdom weekends.

Parishes in the future ought to offer ministries that foster family life, the primal experience of community. Common Sense Parenting is a program that we have worked with for many years, offering parents easily learned skills for effective parenting. Similarly, Marriage Encounter, 10 Great Dates, and The Second Half of Marriage for empty nester marriages are programs that can be held at the parish to foster qualitative and enduring marital relationships that bring the happiness we talked about earlier.

We must not forget the large group of people in most of our congregations and parishes that are single, either by choice or circumstance. Our Pathways ministry reaches out to and offers various spiritual, social, and educational opportunities for those who are single.

Some ten years ago, in cooperation with the Adler School of Professional Psychology, we opened a psychological services center on the grounds of the parish. Master's-level and doctoral-level students have done *practica*, or internships, offering our parishioners educational and therapeutic services at a reduced financial rate. This center is now being re-imagined under a new title, the Center for Inner Peace, Hope, Forgiveness, and Reconciliation. This new ministry is offering educational programs on anxiety management, on the transformation of depression, and on forgiveness (which I frequently run because I did my doctoral work on the psychology of forgiveness), as well as seminars on reconciliation for the building up of trust in relationships where that trust has been broken. The center also offers Rising from Divorce, an educational series for adults and children in the crisis of divorce. The new center will continue to offer individual, group, marital, and family therapy. It will be directed by myself and several parishioners who are psychologists.

In line with the Search Institute, we continually educate our parents on the "40 Developmental Assets," which, if nurtured in children, help teenagers to remain drug-free and alcohol-free, to manage sexuality in a healthy way, to do well in school, and to have healthy minds and bodies. It has become clear to us that the 40 Developmental Assets cannot be started as someone is turning fourteen. Our commitment to the 40 Developmental Assets has challenged us to begin educating parents on the Assets when their children are in the early childhood years. We will return to the Assets in the chapter on family-based evangelization.

A MOMS ministry gathers young mothers on Wednesday mornings to deal with topics of interest. With all of these ministries, an effective nursery ministry, which cares for children while parents are involved in one of the programs or are at worship, is very important.

At a recent joint meeting it was recommended that the nursery ministry expand into a a more comprehensive child care ministry to help parents with children through sixth grade. The current nursery is limited to caring only for toddlers.

One of the most effective ministries that we have sponsored at Holy Family is our Marriage Preparation ministry. The foundational text that we use now is *Unitas*. As with most of our sacramental catechesis, Marriage Preparation is based on an RCIA-like journey model of gradual conversion and transformation. I would say that 95 percent of those who go on this journey come out on the other side enriched, having truly enjoyed the experience with mentoring couples sharing with them the realities of living the sacrament and covenant of marriage.

A marriage preparation ministry can be extremely challenging, given the number of couples now living together before marriage. We have also begun a new ministry based on research at Creighton University published under the title *Time, Sex, and Money: The First Five Years of Marriage.* Called the Honeymooners, the ministry attempts to gather couples regularly during their first five years of marriage. Those in the first five years of marriage remain the only group among the married that still shows a rise in divorce. The rates have leveled off for other age groups. Creighton University's study found that among the major issues challenging young marrieds are debt brought into the marriage by one or both partners; sexual dissatisfaction with each other, usually after having lived with each other before marriage; and time starvation — not having enough time for the relationship, given other demands like work.

A parish ought to help people live. We know what the deepest hungers and thirsts of the human heart are. They are issues that directly relate to happiness and to connection with one's fellow human beings. Rather than continuing in the status quo of what Tony Campolo has called organizational or methodological frozenness, parish leaders ought to listen to the real-life needs of the people connected with their parish or organization, and either create or find ministries that address those needs.

Healthy Parishes

How can a parish, the church, or any organization achieve the health that I am discussing in this chapter, or become centers where people might grow in such health and wholeness? I think we can find some direction in the secular world's assessment of great organizations.

I have been struck by the work of Jim Collins in his best seller *Good to Great.* Collins writes that the greatest enemy of an organization becoming great is a complacency with the status quo, or a complacency with being good, or pretty good. Among Collins's findings regarding great organizations are the following:

1. *Leadership.* To move a good organization toward greatness requires leaders who are self-effacing, quiet, reserved, perhaps even shy. But they also have a paradoxical blend of personal humility and professional will. They have spines of steel. They are more like Lincoln and Socrates than Patton or Caesar, says Collins. They don't have big personalities or make headlines and become celebrities. They have a selfless dedication to the good of the organization or the movement.

2. *First Who, Then What.* Collins found that great leaders "get the right people on the bus, the wrong people off the bus, and the right people in the right seats of the bus." They operate out of the principle that *the right people in the right seats are your most important asset.* Collins's wisdom should be taken into account as we contemplate the growth of pastoral staffs.

3. *Confronting the Brutal Facts, Yet Never Losing Faith.* Great organizations maintain unwavering faith that they can and will prevail in the end, regardless of difficulties. At the same time,

they have the discipline to confront the most brutal facts of current realities, whatever those facts might be.

4. *The Hedgehog Concept.* Using metaphors from the short story *The Hedgehog and the Fox* by Sir Isaiah Berlin, Collins maintains that great organizations resemble hedgehogs more than foxes. The hedgehog is a homely creature, unlike the sleek fox. The fox, with all of his ability, often dashes about, but accomplishes little. The hedgehog knows that he does one thing well. He keeps a den for his family, and he goes about that task with diligence. Building on this metaphor, Collins encourages organizations to practice simplicity in doing what they are best at, to engage in that which they are passionate about, and to be sensitive to what drives their economic engine. The hedgehog principle also stresses the virtue of persistence.

5. *A Culture of Discipline.* Many companies and organizations do not have a culture of discipline. When you have disciplined people, you do not need hierarchy. When you have disciplined thought, you do not need bureaucracy. When you have disciplined action, you do not need excessive controls. When you combine a culture of discipline with an ethic of entrepreneurship, you get the magic alchemy of great performance. Later in the book I will speak of a ministerial discipline that, ideally, all ministries strive to follow at Holy Family. It is a discipline that I have taught and lived for the last thirty years of my priesthood, one that arose out of the doctor of ministry program that I was part of in the late 1970s and early 1980s.

6. *Technology.* For Collins, technology and the addition of technology should never be an end in itself. What is more important is getting the five previous values in place and in practice. Then the importing of mission-appropriate technology accelerates the movement of the organization toward greatness.

As I write this book, I am aware that the parish school in the parish where I grew up is one of twenty-three archdiocesan schools targeted for closure in the Archdiocese of Chicago. My home parish,

St. Thomas More, was one of the thriving parishes of the 1950s, 1960s, and 1970s. The parochial school was booming with children. Multiple vocations to the priesthood emerged from the parish.

But then, in the 1980s, the neighborhood began to change racially and ethnically. Many of the founding fathers and mothers of the parish moved from the southwest side of the city to the southwest suburbs. Little was done to tend to the emerging African American population of the neighborhood. The physical plant of the parish, however, was kept in impeccable shape. Tridentine Latin Masses began to be offered on the weekend, as well as during the week, which attracted a non-neighborhood crowd of conservative Catholics who drove to drink in this restorationist liturgical culture. There were no attempts to evangelize people in the neighborhood. Schoolchildren were expected to attend Tridentine Masses during the week.

Many African Americans interested in Catholicism have abandoned St. Thomas More and gone to a thriving Catholic parish nearby, St. Sabina's. All around St. Sabina's once flourishing parishes have closed and have been either shuttered or sold to Protestant congregations. It breaks my heart to know that the school that I attended as a child, with my brother, where somewhere around seventeen hundred children were educated, now has less than two hundred in the school. The school will close. Rumor is the parish will eventually be closed.

As director of the archdiocesan Office for Chicago Catholic Evangelization, I responded in the 1980s to some parishioners' requests to try to revitalize ministries at St. Thomas More. The pastor, begrudgingly, allowed me to run a regional RCIA there. But when parishioners began to ask for more services and I tried to respond positively to them, he reported me to the Chancery Office, saying that I was overstepping my bounds and threatening his pastorate. After his death, subsequent pastors continued his restorationist ways, resulting in the crisis in that parish, and many other parishes, in the archdiocese.

With no training in the seminary for practical evangelization and no serious attempts at evangelization, especially in urban areas, congregations continue to dwindle in the Archdiocese of Chicago, and many other dioceses.

The research in evangelization over the past twenty or thirty years has shown that truly evangelizing parishes offer worship that, more often than not, is a religious experience; homilies that offer people a livable spirituality; ministries that touch real-life needs; and congregations that are welcoming and embracing. These are the kinds of parishes and congregations that will thrive in the future. Others will gray, age, and, perhaps, close.

Stephen Covey's book *The 8th Habit,* mentioned above, discusses the notion of "voice." That image needs to be expanded and explained. Fr. Donald Cozzens, writing in *Faith That Dares to Speak,* discusses voice in the context of church life. He calls Catholics, both lay and ordained, to raise their voices to help "excavate a Church that is buried alive in a culture of obeisance." Cozzens warns that, at times, even lay people are being co-opted into promoting the status quo of the institutional church, rather than serving the gospel and the faithful.

Cozzens says that an issue needing immediate intervention is the suffocating dynamics that are now present in the church. We still live with an idolatry of the institutional church. Often, believers are blind to all that is really going on around them relative to church. He calls for a holy alliance between priests and laity, recognizing a widening rift between the bishops and everyone else.

Cozzens asserts that one of the problems with the church today is that everybody wants to change the church in his or her own way. There is very little silence in the church. There is too much shrillness, as different factions try to make their arguments heard.

According to Cozzens we ought not to be trying to convince each other, complaining about each other, or protesting against each other, but rather engaging with each other. He talks about the importance of humility in approaching the future church. He calls the church to "contemplative conversation" rather than noisy discourse. This contemplative conversation could lead us into greater experiences of what we talked about earlier: true communion with each other.

Covey further helps us to understand what finding voice could look like. He quotes extensively from a Harris poll that surveyed twenty thousand U.S. residents employed full-time in key industries, in key functions. The statistics that Covey presents highlight that it is not just the Catholic Church that is a dysfunctional environment in which to work. High percentages of people in our nation's industries and corporations report dissatisfaction in their employment with regard to issues like these:

- Lack of a clear sense of the organization's mission
- Lack of clear-cut and measurable goals
- Lack of empowerment in the workplace
- Low levels of trust
- Poor communication
- Little tolerance of opinions differing from those in leadership
- Little accountability for results
- Little cooperation in working relationships

Against this negative context in the lives of many working people, Covey advocates the development of personal voice. Personal voice, he says, is a way to move toward personal and organizational greatness. Voice, he says, is equivalent to personal significance, which we employ in the face of challenge.

Voice is the convergence of need (including what the world needs enough to pay you for), talent (natural gifts and strengths, focused discipline), passion (doing what we love to do, those things that naturally energize, excite, motivate, and inspire), and conscience (that still small voice within that assures us of what is right and prompts us to actually do it). Covey encourages his readers to look at the primary roles in our lives, and about each role to ask the following four questions:

1. What *need* do I sense in my family, my community, and the organization that I work for?

2. Do I possess a true *talent* that, if disciplined and applied, can meet that need?

3. Does the opportunity to meet the need tap into my *passion*?

4. Does my *conscience* inspire me to take action and become involved?

Covey says that there are two roads that people can take in life: the road of finding your voice leading to greatness and, having found your voice, inspiring others to find theirs; or the road to losing voice, moving toward a life of mediocrity, and not helping others to discover theirs.

As with Covey's other seven habits, the eighth habit of voice happens through the convergence of knowledge, a change of attitude, the learning of skills, all moving toward a habit, or a *habitus,* a habit of the heart.

Covey's notion of voice comes from his working paradigm of the "Whole Person." Organizations need to relate to people through the paradigm of the Whole Person. The Whole Person is the convergence of body, mind, heart, and spirit. Each of these components has four intelligences: physical intelligence, mental intelligence, emotional intelligence, and spiritual intelligence. Voice is the fullest expression of spiritual intelligence.

Symptoms of organizations that do not allow voice include bloated costs, inflexibility, slowness, failure in the marketplace, and, eventually, a negative cash flow. In some situations where voice is not encouraged, people within the organization openly rebel or quit. Some stay, with a kind of malicious obedience and complicity and complacency.

Environments encouraging voice have people who work with cheerful cooperation, heartfelt commitment, and creative excitement. Voice provides people with feelings of integrity and a great sense of meaning and of contributing to people and causes. One of the outcomes of voice is *legacy,* working with others in making a genuine contribution to the world around us. Covey's notion of legacy has parallels in Erik Erikson's classical understanding of adult generativity.

Contemplative Conversations

"Contemplative conversations" can be a means of finding voice, and helping one another find voice, in a stifling church. Here we will look at a couple of examples of issues that might be discussed under the rubric of "contemplative conversations."

The Greek Orthodox Church is in the process of restoring women's deaconate, or the role of deaconess. There were women deacons in the church up until the early Middle Ages. This is a matter of history. Even though we are not in official communion with the Greek Orthodox Church, because of the similarity of our theologies we do recognize Greek Orthodox sacraments. If the Greek Orthodox Church is at the point of restoring women to the deaconate, might this become a conversation point around which informed Catholic people might give voice on the issue of restoring women to such a position in the Western church? Might this be an occasion to discuss the role of women in the church in general? If we ever got to a point of actually restoring women to the deaconate in the Roman Catholic tradition, wouldn't that be a liberating position to be in regarding the role of women in the church?

The Roman Catholic Church has accepted married male Lutheran ministers and married male Episcopalian priests into the Roman Catholic priesthood. Why have we done that? And if we have ordained a few married men, why can't we ordain many? And why should ordained priests be deprived of the gift of marriage if it is given to some others? We need to discover voice and to demand, respectfully, conversations about these and other questions. Again, we ought not to be silenced. Rather, informed, intelligent Catholics can no longer sit with closed mouths. We ought not to be infantilized. We ought not to be rendered voiceless and complacent.

Sr. Joan Chittister, O.S.B., raises other issues for contemplative conversations in her February 5, 2005, *National Catholic Reporter* article, "From Where I Stand: Keeping the Eucharistic Community Eucharistic." Sr. Joan documents the aging of the priesthood and the emerging shortage of priests. She speaks of people's deprivation of the Eucharist that this trend is creating. She mentions that out of the twenty rites of the Catholic Church, only the Latin rite (Rome) imposes mandatory celibacy for its priests. She wrestles with the ordination of non-Catholic clergy and the discrimination against men who have been lifetime Catholics, are married, and would be wonderful priests.

She notes the activity of the National Priests' Council of Australia as that group discovers its voice. The priests wonder why the pre-occupation of bishops and cardinals relative to liturgy has been on the standardization of rubrics and detailed instructions, while many communities around the world are deprived of the Eucharist because of the priest shortage and mandatory celibacy for priests. The priests call the bishops of the world to deal with five issues:

1. The enculturation of Eucharistic practices

2. The extension of ordination to single men of good character who would preside at the Eucharist within their own communities so that the opportunity to celebrate is reasonably available

3. The extension of ordination of married ministers from other Christian traditions to Roman Catholic men

4. The appropriateness of insisting upon obligatory celibacy for priests

5. The reinstatement of priests who married with the church's permission and are willing to resume ministry as priests

They do not speak of the ordination of women. Sr. Joan wonders whether their theology is lacking, or they are just politically wise.

At Holy Family we offer a series of Contemplative Conversations seasonally, in the fall and during Lent. Our evenings begin with some simple instructions on prayer, meditation, and contemplation. Twenty minutes of prayer follows after the topic of the evening has been announced. Individuals are encouraged to pray for the direction of the Holy Spirit and wisdom relative to the assigned topic.

This period of prayer, or contemplation, is followed by a teaching on the topic for the evening. The official magisterial position is presented, as well as contemporary theological reflection. The presentation lasts approximately thirty minutes. The final half hour is given to open microphones scattered throughout the church where individuals can come up and state opinions or ask questions in a town hall meeting fashion. No comment should exceed three minutes.

The evening closes in small groups, in fifteen-minute discussions on "Where do we go from here?" and "How should we respond to our experience this evening?" Each of the groups makes written recommendations to the parish staff and Pastoral Council for further reflection, discernment, and action. Part of the action, I believe, should involve a sharing of the news with the local ordinary of any parish or alliance that might try this, so that he, and indeed bishops in general, are more in touch with the movement of the Holy Spirit among their people.

Recent Contemplative Conversations in our series have included "Racism in America" (with Michael Pfleger), "Gospel Living in American Culture" (with Joan Chittister), "The Priesthood: A Vocation in Crisis" (with Andrew Greeley), "Taking Back Our Church" (with Robert Kaiser), and "What Jesus Meant by the Reign of God" (with John Dominic Crossan).

We are grateful to Donald Cozzens and Stephen Covey for helping our parish discover how we might better find voice.

Chapter Three

Creating a Relational Net

O NE OF MY HEROES in evangelization work is Dr. Paul Cho, who has worked for years in Seoul, South Korea, networking tens of thousands of people in small house churches. His work has been popularized in the United States by Dr. John Hurston and his daughter, Karen Hurston.

Building on the imagery that Jesus uses in the gospel that he will make his disciples "fishers of people," Cho has written and spoken extensively about the work of evangelization as that of creating a relational net that "catches" people. The notion of "catching people" is not meant in a manipulative sense, but rather in an invitational sense. Cho feels that through networks of relationships, specifically inviting people into membership in small groups and house churches, evangelization can be made real, practical, and down-to-earth. He also teaches that if any congregation or parish is missing a significant demographic group, there is an evangelical hole in that church's net that needs attention and mending.

Dr. Cho has likewise created a mentoring or coaching system, whereby all small group leaders are provided resources by people experienced in the dynamics of small group life. These mentors also have direct access to the pastor; thus a communication system is created between all the small groups and what we understand in Catholic culture as the pastor and pastoral staff. This mentoring and coaching system is an attempt to achieve quality control of the materials being used in the small groups, as well as of the style and quality of pastoring being done by the small group leaders.

In my work as evangelization director for the Archdiocese of Chicago in the 1980s and 1990s, I developed a strong interest in small

groups as the best means for ongoing spiritual growth and evangelization for adults. I have studied many Catholic and Protestant models
that have successfully used small Christian communities as a means
of ongoing faith formation after people have experienced primary, or
foundational, evangelization.

At the Office for Chicago Catholic Evangelization, Dawn Mayer
and I began to provide resources for parishes that had been in the
Renew process for two and a half years, and wanted to continue the
experience of small group life. Our initial offering was called "Parish Spirituality," a series of faith-sharing booklets, the last of which
was a training booklet on how to continue Small Christian Communities without an archdiocesan office producing materials for you. I
also have taught in many graduate school ministry programs on the
theology, spirituality, and discipline of Small Christian Communities.

The greatest satisfaction that I have found in ministry has been as
the pastor of a large parish, Holy Family. I was brought on to the
parish staff as a part-time consultant and sacramental minister. My
consulting work was to be in the areas of Small Christian Communities, the RCIA, and ministry formation. I began this work in 1992
part-time and went on to embrace it full-time as coordinator of EST
(Evangelization, Stewardship, and Training). In 1992 I began to try to
deepen and improve the quality of RCIA efforts at the parish. In 1993
I began working with a core community commissioned by the Pastoral Council to investigate and initiate Small Christian Communities.
The parish leadership decided that it did not want simply to operate
multiple programs, as was idealized in the 1970s and 1980s. Rather,
Holy Family wanted to become a network of genuine communities.

Working a Process

In the early 1990s, Holy Family was not a stranger to Small Christian Communities. There were a number of groups attempting small
group sharing. Some groups met as reunion groups after an initial
retreat experience at the parish called Kingdom weekends. Over the
years, some people had gathered in homes for faith sharing during
the Lenten season. But there was no ongoing development of Small

Christian Communities toward a paradigm shift in which the parish would become a network of Small Christian Communities. That work began in the summer of 1993.

As I work with parishes around the country and around the world, I emphasize, on the basis of our experience at Holy Family, the importance of *working a process* with the congregation. The process ensures education and formation of both leaders and parishioners with regard to any innovation, such as Small Christian Communities, that is being attempted.

Working a process involves *talking to opinion makers.* Opinion makers include most folks in the parish, so process work must be widespread. In working such a process, those leading the innovation or paradigm shift must see that communal, shared values are not trampled upon or in any other way shown disrespect. In fact, those working toward the innovation must show how the new model, in this case Small Christian Communities, actually shares in traditionally held values of the parish. Working a process toward a paradigm shift must convince people at large that the parish will be better because of the new effort. Part of working the process is to launch a successful pilot, and as the pilot is evaluated as successful, to then move on to enhance the innovation.

Our process toward Small Christian Communities involved studying many models, nationally and internationally. I had some of this research at my fingertips after having written on and taught about Small Christian Communities for years. Holy Family at this time was still part-time work for me; I was still working full-time at the time at the Institute of Pastoral Studies as the coordinator of the Center for Evangelization, Catechesis, and Religious Education. From that position I networked with six other parishes and Holy Family. The seven parishes, of quite diverse socioeconomic backgrounds, became the Communal Parish Project. We worked to support each other in starting small groups for over a year. After we launched our respective pilots, the network did not stay together very long.

One of the ways that we tried to talk to and listen to opinion makers and draw people into small communities at Holy Family was to have two informational/formational evenings on Small Christian

Communities prior to Lent of 1994. Our first evening was called "Back to the Future." It was a night of renewal on the style of church exemplified in the second chapter of the Acts of the Apostles, with special attention to the reference that these first Christians went daily to the Temple (large church) and also met in each other's homes for the breaking of bread and for prayer (Small Christian Communities). While over a thousand invitations were sent, only about sixty-five people attended.

A second evening was offered in January. This was an actual experience of a lectionary-based gathering. About fifty attended. From that mix of sixty-five and fifty came our first group of facilitators for training. We trained our first facilitators in *human relations skills:* how to listen; showing empathy, or reflecting back people's feelings; drawing out introverts and toning down people who dominate conversation; leading group discussion and faith sharing. Today we still provide this level of training as well as training in *basic skills with scripture:* how to read scripture in a non-fundamentalist way; how to do exegesis, trying to understand the intent of the author and the viewpoint of the audience to which the author was speaking; how to understand the historical background connected with the passage of scripture; how to engage in hermeneutics, or the interpretation of scripture for our own day.

Small Christian Community Meetings

In putting together our first materials we carefully crafted the steps for an evening. For the last eleven years we have produced our own lectionary-based faith-sharing materials in a booklet entitled *Sharing Faith*. To begin the meetings we borrowed from an Episcopalian small group process, *The Word*, the step of "Coming Aboard and Welcoming," approximately ten minutes of sharing on the nature of each individual's day. Ten minutes was added for Centering Prayer to contextualize the gathering in prayerfulness.

I was impressed many years ago by Roberta Hestenes, who taught for some time at Fuller Theological Seminary. Hestenes emphasized the importance of an emerging covenant among the members of the group. Thus, the pioneers of Holy Family's Small Christian Communities decided to close Centering Time with the recitation of the Covenant Prayer. Each group is given permission to articulate their own covenant prayer. We also have a standard one, which any of the groups can use. The standard Covenant Prayer contains key elements that the small group needs, if it is going to grow and endure as a group.

COVENANT PRAYER

(To be prayed together at each meeting)

Thank you, God, for this opportunity
to be in this group,
an important part of the total Body of Christ.
Help us to pray, share life, and share scripture
with each other.
Help us to minister to each other,
the larger parish, and the world.
Help us also in our commitment to each other:
to be here as often as we can,
to share with each other from the heart,
to respect confidentiality,
and to be church with and for each other.
May the covenant bond that exists
among us as a group, between us and You,
our great God, grow and deepen each time
that we are with each other.
We ask this through Christ our Lord.
Amen.

The next step of a small group meeting we call Review of the Week. It has popularly become known as "God Sightings." For thirty minutes, participants in the group are encouraged to tell stories of how they sensed the movement or presence of God since the group last met. At this stage of small group sharing, people can share personal experience, events in the news, or events in the church or in the parish. The key question is this: "Does anyone feel, sense, hear, or intuit the voice, the movement, the will of God in the events of our lives?" This section of our small group sharing was borrowed from a model developed at the Lumko Missiological Institute in South Africa under the influence of Fritz Lobinger. In the Lumko materials, this step is called "Look at Life."

The group then tends to next Sunday's readings. Five or six questions for "Breaking Open the Word" are included in the *Sharing Faith* booklet for each week. An additional question always points to the mercy or social justice implications of the scripture passages. Before getting to the faith-sharing questions, the scripture is proclaimed. At this point also, a video can be played. As pastor, I do exegesis and hermeneutics of the scriptures for fifty-two weeks of readings. I borrowed this idea from St. Boniface Parish in Pembroke Pines, Florida, where the pastor, Michael Eivers, connected with his parishioners in their homes through the use of the VCR. I tell small group leaders that they can play all or part of the video for their small group, or just use it as a personal resource for themselves in getting ready to lead the group. We are in the process of acquiring the technology to do this piece on DVDs.

After about thirty minutes of "Breaking Open the Word," the next stage the group enters is called "A Look at the Future — Responding." In this stage, group participants talk about how they are going to try to live out what was shared in the small group. Other issues looked at include how the group can influence society, based on the group's sharing. Some groups that have been with each other for awhile are involved in either mercy or justice projects and share at this point on how they are progressing with their projects.

A movement toward mercy and justice is vital for small group life. Many groups that just stay on the level of spiritual self-nurture tend to run out of energy or passion. The works of mercy and justice keep a group passionate and alive. Thirty minutes are given to this "Look at the Future." This stage was also borrowed from an African model. In the Lumko materials, this stage is called "Love" (How Can We Lovingly Put the Gospel into Action?).

The group meeting concludes with prayerful petitions. Here we follow the advice of Lyman Coleman, who has been a leader in small group work for years, that the least threatening way of praying in a group is through petitions. The petitions are brought to a close through the recitation of the Lord's Prayer. Borrowing a gesture from St. Boniface parish, we encourage our groups in this prayer time to join hands and form a circle facing outward toward the doors and the windows. Symbolically this is an attempt to send each other forth from the place of comfort and security, which is the small group, to be salt, light, and leaven for the world.

Supporting Small Groups

As part of working our process toward small groups, I preached on a new way of being and doing church a couple of times before Lent of 1994. When it finally came time to sign up for small groups, over five hundred people committed themselves to the process.

We do sign-up for small groups three times a year, beginning with fall small group sharing, with a six-week series ending before Advent begins (see the sign-up card on the following page). There is another sign-up for Lenten small groups, and a third for summer small groups. Those who sign up for seasonal small groups know that they are signing up for a limited contract, but when the contract is completed the small group is encouraged to discuss whether all or some want to continue meeting. Thus, we have seasonal groups and year-round groups meeting regularly. As of this writing, we have approximately fifteen hundred people in approximately 150 small groups.

Every year we offer the Small Christian Community Institute, in which we invite speakers to provide resources for the small community facilitators and members. We also have sessions for small group skills training for both new and experienced group leaders. A couple of times a year, we have a gathering of all small groups for a shared meal. Connected with one of those meals in the summer is what we call our Courtyard Mass. We gather for liturgy in a beautiful courtyard that is part of our campus, and then a meal follows. We have found it to be vital to get small groups facilitators and members together on an occasional basis for support and to learn from each other. As pastor, I visit groups on a regular basis and also meet with

Sign Up to Join a –
SMALL CHRISTIAN COMMUNITY – FAITH SHARING GROUP

SHARING
OUR FAITH
Small Christian Communities

Holy Family Parish
2515 W. Palatine Road
Inverness, IL   60067
847-359-0042

I WOULD LIKE TO JOIN A SMALL CHRISTIAN COMMUNITY
✓ *Check one option below…*

I would like to join a SCC group.

I would like to lead a SCC group.
(Training will be provided)

Name _____

Address _____

Town/Zip _____

Phone (home) _____

Phone (work) _____

Email _____

Mini-Parish _____

Identify preferred day and time to meet…

1 – 1st choice	Day of the Week
2 – 2nd choice	S M Tu W Th F Sa
Choose: (1, 2 or 3)	Choose: (Day of Week)

Morning _____   _____

Afternoon _____   _____

Evening _____   _____

*Please bring this card to the appropriate
table in the narthex or
return to Holy Family Parish office.*

1-05   (over)

SMALL CHRISTIAN COMMUNITY – FAITH SHARING GROUP

Choose from the following options:

Faith Sharing Groups
☐ *Sharing Faith* Booklet
   Lectionary, Sunday Readings Based

Awareness Groups
☐ *Faith That Dares to Speak,* Donald Cozzens
☐ *The 8th Habit*, Stephen Covey
☐ *The Five People You Meet in Heaven*, Mitch Albom
☐ *The Problem of Pain*, C. S. Lewis
☐ *The Purpose Driven Church*, Rick Warren
☐ *The Purpose Driven Life,* Rick Warren
☐ *The Question of God*, Dr. Armand M. Nichols, Jr.
☐ *The Way of Forgiveness*, Patrick J. Brennan
☐ *Why I Am Catholic*, Garry Wills

☐ Civic Responsibility: What's It All About?
☐ Christian Prayer: Deepening My Experience of
   God, 12 sessions)
☐ Embracing Life
☐ Grieving the Death of a Loved One
☐ Life in Christ: Walking With God (12 sessions)
☐ Making God Visible: Parenting You r Children
☐ Nurturing Our Commitment,
   The Early Married Years
☐ Strengthening Family Life
☐ The Celebration of the Christian Mystery:
   Sacraments (12 sessions)

clusters of facilitators. We are also extending an invitation for home Masses to small groups or clusters of small groups. These efforts are an attempt to assure quality control in our Small Christian Communities. Speaking ecclesiologically, small groups need to be reminded always that they are connected with larger church organisms, namely, the parish, the diocese, and the universal church.

Our Small Christian Community facilitators are commissioned yearly at one of our large Sunday Masses, usually the 9:00 a.m. Sunday Mass. Through the commissioning, we are tying to educate the congregation that the ministry of the Small Christian Community facilitator is as vital and needed as that of other ministries that are liturgically commissioned (e.g., catechists, Eucharistic ministers, lectors).

In addition to producing our own faith-sharing booklet and videotape, we have also provided facilitators with other resources. Each small group facilitator receives a copy of *Quest,* a faith-sharing booklet from the diocese of Hartford, Connecticut; *Living the Word,* produced by World Library/Paluch Publications; and *Sunday by Sunday,* produced by Good Ground Press. Should the materials we produce be weak for a given session, I want our leaders to feel they are sufficiently prepared.

Awareness Groups

After nine years of a lectionary-based program, we decided to borrow from Lobinger's Lumko materials and encourage some small groups to become *Awareness groups.* Awareness groups, for one or more six-week periods, make use of resources in addition to the Sunday scriptures. Most of our Awareness groups have also allotted twenty to thirty minutes of their meeting to what we call "Faith First." I will explain Faith First more in depth later. Suffice it to say at this point that Awareness groups choose one of the readings, usually the Gospel, and share one or two faith-sharing questions focused on it. They do not go through all the steps of a typical group meeting as discussed earlier.

Awareness groups usually concentrate on popular spiritual reading. The leaders are encouraged to divide the number of chapters by six weeks and cover that number of chapters each session. These are the questions used to discuss the books:

1. What struck you most from this week's assigned reading?

2. Why do you think it struck you?

3. What ideas do you find most challenging in the assigned material?

4. Was there any material you do not understand that the group could help you with?

5. Is there any part of the material you find difficult to accept or agree with?

6. What, from the assigned material, do you find memorable? What do you think you will remember and carry within you in the future?

Books we have used over the last several years include:

• *The Question of God* by Armand M. Nicholi Jr.

• *Power of Intention* by Wayne Dyer

• *Brave New Church* by William Bausch

• *God Alone Suffices* by Slawomir Biela

• *Speaking My Mind* by Tony Campolo

• *Leadership on the Line* by Ronald A. Heifetz and Martin Linsky

• *Good to Great* by Jim Collins

• *The Heart of Christianity* by Marcus J. Borg

• *Familiar Stranger* by Michael McClymond

• *The Call to Discernment in Troubled Times* by Dean Brackley

• *Anger* by Thich Nhat Hanh

• *The Problem of Pain* by C. S. Lewis

• *The Five People That You Meet in Heaven* by Mitch Albom

• *The Purpose Driven Life* by Rick Warren

+ *The Purpose Driven Church* by Rick Warren
+ *The Way of Forgiveness* by Patrick Brennan

Challenges Facing Small Christian Communities

One of the things that I have worked on, so that Small Christian Communities are not dependent on me and hopefully will survive when I am no longer pastor, is the Core Community. The Core Community is a Small Christian Community that has taken on responsibility for the continuation of Small Christian Communities, for the proliferation of Small Christian Communities, and for the continuing paradigm shift toward true community for the entire parish. The group also provides other services, like ensuring ongoing training and formation, communication between and among small groups through a newsletter, the processing of new small group members, and the placement of new members in small groups.

A very important role the Core Community plays is that of mentor or liaison. Each of our Core Community members takes the responsibility of being a contact for approximately ten small groups and their leaders. This regular checking in on small groups and their leaders is another means of communication, quality control, and problem intervention.

Contained in each *Sharing Faith* booklet are two resources in addition to the steps of the small group meeting. An in-depth evaluation form is enclosed to help the group evaluate itself in the areas of faith sharing; support of each other; quality of prayer; openness to ministry, mercy, and justice; and other group-related issues. Many who have done research into small group life have discovered that life in a small community is like a marriage or a family. Issues, feelings, problems, and responsibilities need to be discussed openly. If these are swept under the rug, the group will begin to have difficulties that only will become worse if they are not discussed.

Also in the book are the words to songs sung at weekend liturgies. If the group is comfortable with singing, we encourage it as part of group prayer.

As pastor and also as one of those involved in leadership in Small Christian Communities, I try to meet with groups of facilitators at least once a month. At these meetings I remind the facilitators of our history and of our small group methodology for lectionary-based groups and Awareness groups. Then the lay leader of the Small Christian Communities and I spend time listening to the leaders, their successes, their challenges. In this exchange, facilitators pick up good ideas and tips from one another.

A recurring problem for us is people who drop out of small groups after a few meetings, or people who sign up for small groups but then don't show up for the first meeting. We are brainstorming as to how we might reach out to people to more effectively bond people together in small groups. We believe that we need to be recruiting people to small groups throughout the year at times other than the three sign-ups we do in church. We feel we also must find more natural ways of gathering people, e.g., shared vocations, neighbors, extended families, friends, or a synthesis of all of these.

We have learned that after a small group sign-up at church, immediate follow-up is vital. If a lot of time passes between sign-up and contact, the potential new member loses interest.

The principal factors determining when and why people have gathered for small groups at Holy Family are *day of the week* and *time of day*. In addition to these connections, the following common interests have also been important: We have had groups for singles, married couples, men, women, young adults, seniors, and parents.

We are also planning to try a taste of small communities immediately following the sign-up after Mass to begin the relationship with a small group with greater immediacy. Again, sometimes if there is a time gap between sign-up and the meeting of the small group, people lose interest or energy.

At a recent meeting one small group facilitator requested that facilitators gather monthly to talk about the scriptures that they will discuss with their small groups. Some facilitators plan to do this. They feel that they can support each other and so better serve their small groups.

Parish Structures

As Small Christian Communities grew in strength, the leaders of Holy Family decided to expand the communal paradigm. With Small Christian Communities successfully initiated, parish leadership turned its attention toward parish governance structures. I will speak more on parish structures in the chapter on parish governance, but I want to touch on the topic here briefly.

Like many parishes in the 1990s, Holy Family operated with a board structure in its governance and ministries. As the parish began a re-imagining of its parish council, that task led us to examine how the parish operated in general. We began to re-imagine parish ministering teams as *Ministering Communities*. That meant whenever any ministering group met, before it did any business, it would do some of what the Small Christian Communities were doing.

We came to understand community as made up of four ingredients: prayer; the sharing of scripture; koinonia, or communion with one another; and service. We decided that every Ministering Community would look at one of the following Sunday's readings, address a faith-sharing question or two, and share some prayers of petition before the group got down to business. This practice of giving about fifteen minutes to faith sharing in our Ministering Communities became known as Faith First, meaning we always intend to engage in faith sharing and in prayer before we get to tasks.

At this time there are 150 Ministering Communities at Holy Family. That means about fifteen hundred people in Small Christian Communities and other groups, and a comparable number in parish ministries, are potentially encountering the Sunday readings before they ever come to the Eucharist. Small Christian Communities have definitely enriched the worship life of the community.

In the mid-1990s Holy Family did not have an effective, meaningful governance structure. We began to build a mini-council model with six mini-councils to govern six major divisions of ministry in the parish. Here also we applied the discipline of community. The mini-councils came to be known as the "Leadership Communities." Those original six Leadership Communities have grown into eight: Adult

Faith Formation; Evangelical Outreach; Worship; Family F.A.I.T.H. and Life; Pastoral Care; Youth Ministry; Operations; and Service, Justice and Peace. Each of the Leadership Communities has a staff pastoral director and/or co-director, associate director, or coordinator assigned to it. The roles of these staff members will be explored later.

The eight Leadership Communities meet on the second Tuesday of the month at 7:00 p.m. for approximately two hours. Here also we employ Faith First at the beginning of each Leadership Community meeting. The monthly meetings rotate agenda. Some meetings are all business. Some meetings are faith formation and business. Some meetings are skills training and business.

Each of the eight Leadership Communities selects a representative to the Pastoral Council, which meets on the third Tuesday of the month at 7:00 p.m. The decision-making style of the Pastoral Council in relationship to the eight Leadership Communities will be discussed in another chapter.

The Family

Having established Small Christian Communities and a communal governance and ministry structure for the parish, we next turned attention to enriching the basic cell of church, the family. Holy Family's child-oriented religious education had been named in the mid-1980s by an acronym, F.A.I.T.H., standing for Faith Alive in the Home. Even though the parish's ideal was that catechesis should focus on the family, the catechesis was still child-oriented, with parents dropping their children off at the homes of catechists.

Slowly over the years we have restructured to evangelize families in and through the evangelization and catechesis of their children. Sacramental preparation for Baptism, Reconciliation, Eucharist, Confirmation, and Marriage was redesigned around an RCIA-like rhythm. Wherever possible, family sessions replaced child-oriented sessions. The family catechetical sessions were connected to one of the weekend liturgies with families coming to worship and staying for a catechetical session, or coming to a catechetical session and staying on for one of the Masses.

Public rituals to mark the beginning of the journey toward the celebration of the sacrament were placed in weekend liturgies. The process delivered the message: the parish is not focused on individuals but rather on family consciousness; the sacrament is not a holy thing to be received but rather a celebration of the ongoing conversion of the individual and also the family that the individual is part of.

A *gradual initiation/family perspective* model of catechesis began to replace the schooling model of catechesis. As the family emphasis began to grow roots, the entire F.A.I.T.H. process became more family-focused. The children's catechesis became lectionary-based, with the year's themes flowing from or connected to the weekend readings. Family activities based on those readings, to be carried out at home, became part of the process. Nights of renewal for families, called Family Foundations, and Faith-Ins were spread throughout the process.

Two parallel processes began to grow out of the model. A shortage of volunteer catechists one year necessitated the creation of a process call F.A.I.T.H., Too. This is a family-based model in which parents catechize their children at home. Children and parents come to the parish campus once a month for family-based religious education. The children attend a child-oriented session, while parents are given training and formation in the next month's sessions that are to be held in the homes. What started as a crisis has become a life-giving and popular version of our catechesis of families.

The second development that has become even more widespread and popular is the Clusters of Families model of religious education. In this model, families in neighborhoods or connected in some other way (e.g., playing on the same sports teams, attending the same school) form the equivalent of an extended family-based Small Christian Community. The parents take turns doing the catechesis with their children. If some parents do not feel called to catechesis, they assume some other ministerial role (e.g., hospitality, administration, prayer ministry). Over half the families of the thirteen hundred children in grades one through six are now in Clusters of Families catechesis.

We are in the process of further expanding Clusters of Families to make it more anchored in weekend Eucharist. In this revision, started last year in the parish, Clusters of Families were encouraged to come to family-based religious education after the 9:00 a.m. liturgy on Sunday. This new effort is called Gathered at Table. In Week 1 of the process, there is large-group adult catechesis while children meet in small learning groups. In Week 2, while the children are in learning groups, the parents are in Small Christian Communities. In Week 3 we celebrate an intergenerational family festival.

A number of F.A.I.T.H., Too families have decided to meet before Mass on the weekends. The paradigm is shifting toward a Eucharist-hubbed family religious education process. This is an example of what William Huebsch means when he says that the parish ought to become the catechist.

The families go into church to celebrate the opening rites of the Mass together, but then all the children are dismissed for Children's Liturgy of the Word. Children's Liturgy of the Word, up to this point an optional part of Family F.A.I.T.H., is now an expected part of Family F.A.I.T.H. Families are being encouraged to choose the liturgy they most frequently attend. This permits catechetical leaders to make the necessary arrangements for space, the number of participants in Children's Liturgy of the Word, catechists, etc.

As catechetical leaders we are clearly trying to say that the Eucharist is the source and summit of our faith. We are trying to get at the catechetical dysfunction identified years ago by master catechist Johannes Hoffinger and by the father of the modern evangelization movement, Pierre Liège. Both lamented a religious education of children that did nothing to help the parents on the journey of conversion, as well as the practice of catechizing children whose families do not worship in a regular fashion.

We have described Gathered at Table as Sabbath-based religious education. As with any innovation there has been some resistance, and there are practical bugs that need to be worked out, for example, parents trying to attend to all of their children's family-based religious education experiences when there are two, three, or four children. We are finding that the only way to do such catechesis is in a multi-grade process, gathering children of different ages into one group while giving individual attention that is developmentally appropriate to each child in small break-out groups. We are piloting such a multi-child effort this year, under the title Faith Alive, on Monday afternoons.

The movement from a schooling model to a gradual initiation of families model of religious education has been the most challenging and slow-moving part of the paradigm shift of evangelizing through the creation of a relational net.

Neighborhood Ministry

Another piece of the relational net has been the establishment of Neighborhood Ministry over the past several years. I have always felt that people needed to be pastored in smaller units than thirty-eight hundred families, or whatever the number for the typical large Catholic parish. Over thirty years ago I began a version of neighborhood ministry in my first parish, as an associate pastor. I have continued neighborhood efforts in all the parishes that I have served in for the past thirty-four years. While it is true that we live in a society where neighborhood relationships have become weak, the physical proximity of people living near or with each other still contains within it evangelical potential.

I was struck by two deaths in Holy Family several years ago, one of a young adult, and another, who lived close to the first, of a man in midlife. The neighbors on the block asked me to come over to lead a prayer service in the home of one of the neighbors. One by one they admitted to me that they had lived next to or across from each other for years and barely talked, but these two tragedies brought them together as neighbors, serving and helping each other in the face of death.

Our Neighborhood Ministry structure is based on a vision and strategies that we learned from the Movement for a Better World. We used an updated version of their materials contained in the small book *A Parish Renewed,* by Arthur Purcaro, O.F.A. In fact, Fr. Purcaro assisted us, both in a parish mission and in training sessions, to execute the renewed plan entitled *New Image of Parish.*

In the *New Image of Parish* strategy, the parish is broken down into more manageable zones. We have come to call these zones "mini-parishes." Each mini-parish has a mini-parish coordinator, and ideally a co-coordinator. The mini-parish coordinators are the overseers of two hundred to three hundred households within their mini-parish. Working with the mini-parish coordinator are a number of neighborhood ministers or representatives within each mini-parish.

The role of the neighborhood minister is to connect with neighbors through home visits, telephone calls, faxes, e-mails, or whatever way is effective in reaching out. The occasion for such contact can be to communicate information about events at the parish (for example, the Advent/Christmas schedule, the Lenten/Easter schedule). Neighborhood ministers are encouraged to try to have one social event and/or a neighborhood Mass each year. Neighborhood ministers are especially to take note of pastoral care needs and communicate those needs to the pastoral care director (for example, someone sick or elderly in need of home visits, support, anointing of the sick, or communion to the sick).

In the purest model of *New Image of Parish,* ministries usually performed at the parish site or on the parish campus begin to be carried out in the mini-parish or the zone. This has happened for Holy Family in the Clusters of Families model of religious education described earlier. Other ministries, like pastoral care of the sick, have also become more neighborhood-based. Some Small Christian Communities are now being formed around neighborhoods. Neighborhood Ministry has grown to the point of neighborhoods choosing symbols and other identifying markers.

Neighborhood activity is most intense during the summer. I pass through the parish celebrating a minimum of twenty neighborhood Masses. Attached frequently to these Masses are family picnics. Every Advent, 90 percent of the parish receives a home visit from neighborhood ministers, with an Advent packet of devotions, inexpensive gifts, and the Advent/Christmas schedule. Neighborhoods have gathered for projects of mercy and compassion in nursing homes and other areas of need.

We have approximately 190 neighborhood ministers, and we feel that we could use 130 more to do the job well. There has been a lot of turnover in Neighborhood Ministry, because often these people are treated shabbily by their neighbors. Neighborhood ministers do not get return phone calls, and at times have been told, "Don't call me again. Don't visit me." I try to challenge neighborhood ministers to "hang in there," for indeed this relational, net ministry is countercultural in a society that has become increasingly alienated and estranged in relationships.

In addition to gathering in the neighborhood, neighborhoods have gathered at our Sunday 9:00 a.m. Mass, and sit and worship with each other as a neighborhood. Neighborhoods also gather at fish fries that are held on Friday evenings during Lent. Central to the vision of *New Image of Parish* is to gather people for non-threatening events. We have found social events and worship to be the types of experiences at which people do not feel threatened.

Historically we have not used neighborhoods as one of the main starting points for generating Small Christian Communities. As I stated before, we are at a point now where we are beginning to see that neighborhoods can be good gathering places for family-based religious education, Bible Study (which has become another piece of our relational net), and Small Christian Communities.

To ensure quality control in our Small Christian Communities, we have benchmarked a number of Protestant evangelical models and their notion of *mentoring or coaching*. The role of the mentor or coach is to pastor or take care of a number of small group leaders, to check on the quality of their Small Christian Communities, and to offer resources to make those experiences more effective and beneficial. We have begun to call this ministry at Holy Family *a liaison ministry*, with the Core Community taking responsibility for a number of Small Christian Communities and their facilitators.

As part of the liaison ministry, I, as pastor, do a couple of things. I offer myself to facilitators at least once a month to have a pastor-to-pastor conversation. At these meetings group leaders bring up challenges and problems they are having in their groups, and they also share with each other what is working well. I also visit individual groups, usually upon invitation from them. We spend an hour to an hour and a half talking about issues that confront their groups.

This year, a priest assisting me in Neighborhood Ministry and I are extending our home Mass ministry to include clusters of Small Christian Communities. We offer to celebrate home Masses throughout the year for Small Christian Communities and neighborhoods. During Advent 2006, a traveling symbol — an empty manger — was brought to each home Mass as we prayed that the spirit of Jesus be reborn in our hearts.

At a recent meeting with a small group, a woman said that her husband would have nothing to do with Small Christian Communities. He was not attracted to a program of sharing faith. What did appeal to him, the woman said, was small group Bible Study.

I reminded the woman that Bible Study groups are yet another piece of the relational net that we use to evangelize at Holy Family. In addition to Small Christian Communities, there are a number of small groups meeting at the parish campus and in parish homes. The contract in a Bible Study group, between and among the members of the group, is quite different from a contract for faith sharing. Faith sharing implies a great deal of personal sharing, not so much on the level of psychological intimacy, but rather on the level of one's personal meaning in life. A contract for Bible Study, while it can include elements of personal sharing, involves rather a shared commitment to learn from a given passage of scripture. Bible Study groups have focused on the Acts of the Apostles, the four Gospels, Paul's Epistles, and other parts of the Bible.

In addition to Bible Study groups, the parish leader of scripture study also leads the Holy Family Catholic Bible School. This is an academic, scholarly study of the scriptures using professional staff and other hired resource persons to offer courses on different books of the Bible. Several years ago, on the Fridays of June and July, I offered a survey course on the Old Testament. I was surprised that over fifty people came out every Friday night, during the summer, to study and learn about the Old Testament. One summer I offered, again on Friday nights, a course entitled "Job: The Problem of Suffering and the Meaning of Life." This past summer I offered a course entitled "The Letters to All Christians." Other systematic courses on different books of the Bible have been offered by other staff members and hired resource persons. A seminar entitled "Bible Journey" is taught by Dr. Jim Papandrea, our director of Adult Formation. This year-long series is offered both during the day and in the evening. These sessions are all very well attended. In this parish church there is a great thirst for knowledge about the Bible.

Bible Study groups and Bible courses "catch" people in that relational net I have spoken about throughout this chapter.

Chapter Four

Family F.A.I.T.H. and Life

JESUS *can* be known. We can come to know the heart and the mind of Jesus. I believe that part of his Reign of God mission was, and is, to teach people to think and feel in renewed ways. Studying the scriptures, especially in the context of community, we can come to know Jesus. As we come to know Jesus, we ought to *live Jesus.* Jesus can never be lived in isolation. Jesus is lived in *community.* These seem to me to be the implicit goals of Catholic religious education, to lead people *to know and live Jesus in the context of community.*

The most basic cell of community, the most basic cell of the Reign of God, is the domestic church of family relationships. The late John Paul II and the U.S. bishops, in the late 1980s and again in the late 1990s, called pastoral ministers to *family consciousness* (see the chart on the following page). Family consciousness challenges us not just to minister to an individual, or focus on an individual, as the society around us does. Family consciousness challenges us to consider *social context,* the network of relationships that a person is a part of. Over the years we have tried to put family consciousness into practice, especially in our religious education efforts.

I mentioned earlier that, gradually, we have transformed Faith Alive in the Home into a family-based model of religious education. This has been slow work. There has been much resistance to it. There is still, in Catholic parenting consciousness, the feeling that "there must be someone other than myself [the parent] who will give my child faith." For the last thirty-four years, in structuring curricula for family-based religious education, and here at Holy Family, I have emphasized that good religious education involves a "love triangle"

FAMILY CONSCIOUSNESS

"No plan for organized pastoral work at any level must ever fail to take into consideration the pastoral area of the family."
—Pope John Paul II, *Familiaris Consortio*, no. 70

A Family Perspective

A family perspective is not a program. It is a perspective . . . a sensitivity . . . a new lens through which to "see" families.

It is a habit of always asking the question — no matter what we are about — how does this affect families . . . blended families, single-parent families, traditional families, childless families?

It is a way to keep remembering . . . we are all part of a family.

Christian Vision of Family

The Christian family has four tasks:

- ✦ To form a community of persons
- ✦ To serve life
- ✦ To participate in the development of society
- ✦ To share in the life and mission of the church

Family as a Developing System

Ministers have been shaped in their attitudes, behaviors, and relationships by the families in which they grew up.

All families have strengths, even the most dysfunctional; it is important to focus on those strengths.

Family Diversity

Ethnic, religious, economic, educational, social, family lifestyle differences.

Every church activity has to be studied in light of how it interrelates with the family; church should support the life-giving activities of the family.

Family Life in Partnership with Institutions

Over time, institutions took over most of the functions which were the responsibilities of families; the result for families is stress.

How do we build life-giving partnerships between families and institutions?

Personal Reflection on Family and Ministry

- ✦ How has my family affected my ministry?
- ✦ How does my ministry affect my family?
- ✦ In what specific ways can I/we improve my/our present ministries to make them more supportive of our home life?
- ✦ What specific steps do I/we need to take to become more effective ministers with families?

of parents, catechists, and parish staff, all working as a collaborative, cooperative team in sharing faith. Parents must become a constitutive part of religious education.

Some key elements in our efforts at renewing catechesis at Holy Family have been the following:

- We have added lectionary-based components to our family experiences. These components have been taken home by the children to be shared during the week with their parents. The lectionary-based materials are constantly pointing the family toward the Eucharist as the source and summit of our faith.

- All sacramental catechesis has been anchored in one of the weekend liturgies. Thus, in preparing for the sacraments, families have been given tastes of what it means to be Catholic, mainly to be part of a Eucharistic community.

- Faith-Ins and Family Foundations or family retreat or renewal experiences have been peppered into the process throughout the years, giving families brief tastes of family education and faith sharing.

- This past year we have added two new efforts. "Community on Wednesday" has provided opportunities for praise music and prayerful educational experiences presided over by trained lay presiders. The focus sessions have been on the importance of Eucharist; the importance of mercy and justice; the importance of being people of praise and thanks. Mini-Retreats for families were also added this past year. The evening begins with a meal, and Mini-Retreat 101 has focused on "What Is Faith?" "What Is Responsible Membership in a Faith Community?" "What Is Stewardship?" The stewardship component has ended in some education on discernment of gifts, calling the family to ministerial involvement in the parish. Mini-Retreat 201, on "Prayer and Spirituality for Families," was piloted this year. This upcoming year we will do Mini-Retreat 301, on "Giftedness and Ministry," and 401 on "Mission and Sharing Our Faith."

- Catechist-based sessions are still offered in the homes and on the parish campus. These sessions have become the least populated part of our process, and parents sending children to such classes have the responsibility of attending the other family-based activities I have mentioned already.

- F.A.I.T.H., Too is a home-based religious education model, giving the parents the ultimate responsibility for catechesis, while providing a monthly education session at the parish, as well as large group family experiences.

- Clusters of Families religious education is an experience of extended Small Christian Communities, with clusters of parents rotating responsibility for the catechesis of their children. If a parent does not feel comfortable in doing catechesis, other ministries (e.g., hospitality, mentoring, sponsoring, decorating for events) can be taken on.

The most challenging family-based, Eucharist-based model that we have been preparing was piloted last year. It is called Gathered at Table. In this model, family-based religious education is offered after the 9:00 a.m. Mass on Sunday morning. We hope to expand opportunities for Gathered at Table to other Mass times. This year Faith Alive will give families with several children the opportunity to do catechesis together on Monday afternoons.

A significant addition to our programming beginning next year will be the "making expected" of Children's Liturgy of the Word. Families are being asked to name the Mass they typically attend. To name this Mass is not a hard and fast promise that that is the Mass they will attend all the time. Whether children are in the Gathered at Table process or another family-based religious education program, all children will be expected to attend Children's Liturgy of the Word. This has been an optional part of our process up until this time.

At Children's Liturgy of the Word, children are called forth after the opening prayer of the Mass. The presider gathers them around the table and explains the readings and the catechesis the children are about to hear. The children are then dismissed and taken to different parts of the complex for a breaking open of God's Word that is developmentally appropriate for their age and grade. Children process in and return to their parents around the time that the gifts are brought to the altar.

In all of these efforts, as a parish and as parish leaders, we are trying to engage in a "medium is the message" process. We are saying that it is normative for us, as Catholics, to do our religious education *as families,* and to do our religious education *in the context of the Eucharist.*

Principles of Family-Based Education

Recently I addressed a group of catechists about my vision and dream for family-based religious education. These are some of the principles I mentioned:

+ Let us remember the goals of religious education:

    – To help people grow in intimacy with the Triune God

    – To know God

    – To help people appropriate the values and attitudes imbedded in the teaching of Jesus Christ about the Reign of God

    – To grow in an interior appropriation of the unfolding tradition of the church

    – To change our behavior with special emphasis on acts of mercy and justice

    – To share in a network of relationships that begins with family and expands to other relational connections in the parish

    – To transform all of the above into a personal, lived spirituality.

+ We have approximately thirteen hundred children in our Family F.A.I.T.H. effort. We will not meet the goals mentioned above unless we better evangelize and catechize not just the children, but also their parents, that is, the family, as the basic cell of church.

- As a parish, and in the Family F.A.I.T.H. process, we have been emphasizing *family consciousness* for years. Family consciousness means that all that we do, we do through the lens of the home, the family from which the children come.

- Our RCIA-like approaches to sacramental catechesis (i.e., the family or engaged couples taking a family journey toward the sacrament, the family meeting with some frequency before or after weekend Eucharist) has been an attempt to move toward this family-based model.

- So also Family Faith-Ins and Family Foundations have contributed to the effort.

- Among the strongest moves toward this model have been F.A.I.T.H., Too and the Clusters of Families effort, as well as Gathered at Table and Faith Alive, which engage parents, either on the individual family level or in clusters of families, in the religious education of their children.

- I believe other moves need to be made soon to improve and deepen our family evangelization and catechesis:

  - We need to expand our Mini-Retreat model, building on the foundational retreats that give families a threshold experience of faith, parish, prayer, and spirituality.

  - Built into the calendar and curriculum, there needs to be gatherings of parents, like in the family cluster model, for regular Small Christian Community style sharing. Among adults, sharing should be on the upcoming Sunday readings, and on the doctrinal topics that the children are learning about. These gatherings could take place simultaneously with the children's session or at another time.

  - As much as possible, occasional "event evangelization" needs to be planned around the liturgical seasons. These events should gather children and parents for learning opportunities and fun activities, and should culminate in a celebration at one of the weekend liturgies.

– The parish, in a sense, has to become the catechist with the people in the parish being evangelized and catechized.

• To make all of the above happen, I believe we need to move toward the building of a Holy Family Center for Children, Youth, and Families, which houses Family F.A.I.T.H. classes and events; F.L.A.M.E. and high-school youth ministry events; young adult events; family formation events; and multipurpose classrooms that are also utilized by the emerging Holy Family Catholic Academy. Our children, families, and catechists need the home, efficiency, and protection that such a center would provide. I estimate the cost to be between $5.5 and $7 million. Design and fund-raising began in the fall of 2005, factoring in also archdiocesan regional school planning. Groundbreaking will be in the spring of 2007, with completion and opening in the fall of 2008.

• We must continue to work at a united approach to the religious education of children and families with two expressions:

– The Holy Family Family F.A.I.T.H. process

– Holy Family Catholic Academy, our parochial school, a grow-a-school project that yearly adds a grade. In the fall of 2006, we will be up to grade five.

• I am suggesting that Small Christian Communities/Family Consciousness represent the model by which we can accomplish evangelization and catechesis effectively. If we do not better evangelize and catechize children and parents, we are simply continuing an ineffective schooling model of religious education that spends time with children, but really perpetuates inactive or under-churched Catholics.

• All families have values. Values are realities that families prize, publicly affirm, and live. If we are to be effective in evangelization and catechesis, then faith and family life must become a family value. Faith must be prized, publicly affirmed, and lived in an observable way.

- In trying to promote Small Christian Communities, we perhaps have reached a "ceiling" in the occasional weekend solicitation to join a pre-Advent, Lenten, or summer group. The next frontier is to tap into the parents' desire for religious education for their children, and to re-imagine calendaring and curriculum to involve parents *and* children in a much more intense communal model.

40 Developmental Assets

I mentioned in the chapter on the parish as a center for health, the importance of the 40 Developmental Assets in helping children and adolescents to grow. The 40 Developmental Assets were put together over some years by the Search Institute. They are markers that help create young people who are learning well, who are not using or abusing substances, who are not engaging in dangerous or violent behavior, and who have an ordered sexuality.

We began our use of the 40 Developmental Assets by taking a survey of some of our junior high and high-school students. The survey revealed a sexually active adolescent population, a population quite regular in the use of alcohol and, in the case of some, illegal drugs. The survey revealed young people who feel distant from their parents and who feel that they are not important to the adults in their lives. The survey revealed young people very invested and involved in competitive sports, but not very committed to regular reading or experience of the arts.

In June 2006, two national organizations sponsored their yearly report card on parents and adults, as judged by teens. In the six years this project has existed, adults and parents have gotten low grades, mostly Cs and Ds, in their relationships with adolescents.

Our interest in the Assets grew out of the Youth Ministry division, but it has become apparent to those of us in leadership that you cannot start growing the Assets in teenagers when they are fourteen. These Assets should be grown and developed from the time of childhood. Thus, training in the 40 Developmental Assets is now given at various sacramental preparation and adult/family education programs in an attempt to help parents of all age groups of children.

40 DEVELOPMENTAL ASSETS
External Assets

Asset Type	Asset Name	Definition
Support	1. Family support	Family life provides high levels of love and support.
	2. Positive family communications	Young person and her or his parent(s) communicate positively, and young person is willing to seek advice and counsel from parent(s).
	3. Other adult relationships	Young person receives support from three or more nonparent adults.
	4. Caring neighborhood	Young person experiences caring neighbors.
	5. Caring school climate	School provides a caring, encouraging environment.
	6. Parent involvement in schooling	Parent(s) are actively involved in helping young person succeed in school.
Empowerment	7. Community values youth	Young person perceives that adults in the community value youth.
	8. Youth as resources	Young people are given useful roles in the community.
	9. Service to others	Young person serves in the community one or more hours per week.
	10. Safety	Young person feels safe at home, at school, and in the neighborhood.
Boundaries and Expectations	11. Family boundaries	Family has clear rules and consequences and monitors the young person's whereabouts.
	12. School boundaries	School provides clear rules and consequences.
	13. Neighborhood boundaries	Neighbors take responsibility for monitoring young people's behavior.
	14. Adult role models	Parent(s) and other adults model positive, responsible behavior.
	15. Positive peer influence	Young person's best friends model responsible behavior.
	16. High expectations	Both parent(s) and teachers encourage the young person to do well.
Constructive Use of Time	17. Creative activities	Young person spends three or more hours per week in lessons or practice in music, theater, or other arts.
	18. Youth programs	Young person spends three or more hours per week in sports, clubs, or organizations at school and/or in the community.
	19. Religious community	Young person spends one or more hours per week in activities in a religious institution.
	20. Time at home	Young person is out with friends "with nothing special to do" two or fewer nights per week.

40 DEVELOPMENTAL ASSETS
Internal Assets

Asset Type	Asset Name	Definition
Commitment to Learning	21. Achievement motivation	Young person is motivated to do well in school.
	22. School engagement	Young person is actively engaged in learning.
	23. Homework	Young person reports doing at least one hour of homework every school day.
	24. Bonding to school	Young person cares about her or his school.
	25. Reading for pleasure	Young person reads for pleasure three or more hours per week.
Positive Values	26. Caring	Young person places high value on helping other people.
	27. Equality and social justice	Young person places high value on promoting equality and reducing hunger and poverty.
	28. Integrity	Young person acts on convictions and stands up for her or his beliefs.
	29. Honesty	Young person "tells the truth even when it is not easy."
	30. Responsibility	Young person accepts and takes personal responsibility.
	31. Restraint	Young person believes it is important not to be sexually active or to use alcohol or other drugs.
Social Competencies	32. Planning and decision making	Young person knows how to plan ahead and make choices.
	33. Interpersonal competence	Young person has empathy, sensitivity, and friendship skills.
	34. Cultural competence	Young person has knowledge of and comfort with people of different cultural/racial/ethnic backgrounds.
	35. Resistance skills	Young person can resist negative peer pressure and dangerous situations.
	36. Peaceful conflict resolution	Young person seeks to resolve conflict nonviolently.
Positive Identity	37. Personal power	Young person feels he or she has control over "things that happen to me."
	38. Self-esteem	Young person reports having a high self-esteem.
	39. Sense of purpose	Young person reports that "my life has a purpose."
	40. Positive view of personal future	Young person is optimistic about her or his personal future.

I hope the reader is getting a sense that the mission driven parish, trying to improve its evangelical relational net, is not always engaged in apparently "churchy" things. We can help people grow in and experience the Reign of God by improving psychological health, communication skills, and relationship skills.

Family Ministries

The home, marriage, and family life are the basic ways most people will or will not experience the Reign of God and the Body of Christ, the church. Therefore, anything we can do to improve the quality of relationships is holy work. The family, rather than just the child, engages in a catechumenate-like journey of conversion in sacramental catechesis. This faith journey process is especially experienced in our marriage preparation work.

On a quarterly basis, couples gather at our 4:30 p.m. liturgy on Saturday afternoons for the Rite of Engagement, which is followed by a dinner and the first of six sessions in the marriage preparation process. At this large group session, the Marriage Preparation Ministering Community, our liturgical ministers, and I give couples an overview of what the journey of marriage preparation will be like.

I especially emphasize the importance of couples having a prenuptial agreement, to engage in what John Gottman calls "the magic five hours" each week. "The magic five hours" are simply five hours the couple promises to give to each other every week of their marriage. The five hours are given to loving goodbyes each day, loving reunions each day, expressed affection each day, gentle touch each day, and a weekly date of two hours. Gottman maintains that if a couple gives five hours a week to their relationship, even troubled, difficult relationships can be successful marriages.

As I do with all the sacraments, but especially in marriage preparation, I stress the following in my presentation: a sacrament is primarily a *vow* or a *pledge*. That was the original meaning of the word *sacramentum*, as borrowed from the Roman military, and propagated by Tertullian. A sacrament is, secondly, a *sign*. The rituals and symbols in sacramental celebrations speak of mystery greater than ourselves. In the Sacrament of Marriage, the vowing and then the living together in love of the couple becomes a sign of the unconditional love of God for all of creation.

Each sacrament is obviously a *ritual,* but perhaps the ritual is the least important of the ingredients or connotations of sacrament. A sacrament does contain some necessary ritualistic time in church. Very importantly, every sacrament, including marriage, begins *a way of life.* I have taught over the last thirty-four years that the way of life that is a healthy, good marriage, is the kind of friendship spoken of by Jesus in the fifteenth chapter of John. In describing his friendship toward the apostles, Jesus says he will lay down his life for them. He has revealed to them who he is; he has related to them as their equal. He has decided for or chosen them. In turn, life ought to be better, ought to bear fruit because of his friendship with them. Jesus' style of friendship, with his apostles and with all of us, is a goal, an ideal for married couples.

Finally, every sacrament, including marriage, involves a *mission to the world.* I tell couples they do not marry just for themselves, but they marry for others. Society ought to be a better experience, the world ought to be a better experience, church ought to be a better experience because a couple is together living the Sacrament of Marriage.

This initial evening is followed by five other meetings that concentrate on issues like communication skills, finances, family planning, extended families, the role of faith and spirituality in a relationship, and human sexuality.

We also hold a special communal celebration of the Sacrament of Reconciliation for engaged couples. This Reconciliation for the engaged is an updating, if you will, of the old squeezing in of a confession before the wedding Mass. We invite couples, family members, and wedding party members to come to these celebrations, in which couples are given time to express sorrow and forgiveness with each other, and God, and experience the church's blessing of forgiveness and absolution.

I like to use these opportunities to share some of my doctoral research on repentance, sorrow, forgiveness, and reconciliation. A synthesis of what I discovered in my research is that forgiving people are less prone to stress, anger, and depression, and reconciliation is a mutual effort at building up trust in a relationship where trust has been violated.

Not only do we want to prepare couples for marriage; we want also to help them grow married. A very simple process that we have implemented at Holy Family is 10 Great Dates, a video series based on a book of the same name, by David and Claudia Arp. We have found 10 Great Dates to be very nonthreatening, especially to men. In 10 Great Dates, couples come to the parish gathering place to look at a very short video. They then retire to various restaurants in the area, with discussion questions based on the video. We have even arranged to have neighborhood restaurants give couples a special discount when they are on a 10 Great Dates night.

The topics for the ten dates are as follows: Choosing a High-Priority Marriage; Learning to Talk; Resolving Honest Conflict; Becoming an Encourager; Finding Unity in Diversity; Building a Creative Love Life; Sharing Responsibility and Working Together; Balancing Your Roles as Partner and Parent; Developing Spiritual Intimacy; and Having an Intentional Marriage.

The Arps's other program, which we have also begun to use, is called The Second Half of Marriage. Through print and video it helps couples understand and grow through the empty nest period, when children have left home and the couple needs to learn to relate to each other again.

I also mentioned earlier Common Sense Parenting. To round out the discussion of that ministry, I list the topics that are covered in that program: Sending Clear Messages; Punishment vs. Teaching; Consequences; Effective Praise; Preventive Teaching; Clear Expectations; Parents Staying Calm; Children Staying Calm; Corrective Teaching; Teaching Self-Control; Teaching How to Make Good Decisions; Family Meetings; Peer Pressure; Helping Children Succeed in School.

Common Sense Parenting is a reduplicative effort. By that I mean some basic training is given to parents who in turn train other parents. Parishioners develop a leader/co-leader Ministering Community approach, which makes Common Sense Parenting, as with every ministry at Holy Family, a ministry that cares for itself without great demands on the staff, but certainly welcoming from the staff animation, empowerment, and consultation.

Chapter Five

Media, Technology, and Communications

THROUGHOUT THIS BOOK I use the metaphor of a relational net to describe the process of catching people through evangelizing ministries. A discussion of the net would be incomplete if we did not take time to focus on evangelizing through the media, technology, and better efforts at marketing.

For the last twenty-five years, I have co-hosted a radio show called *Horizons* with Dawn Mayer, the pastoral associate at Holy Family as well as director of Family F.A.I.T.H. and director of pastoral ministry. The origins of the show go back close to thirty years, when I would take long drives to the south side of Chicago from St. Hubert's Parish in the far northwest suburbs. I drove home on Sundays for dinner and to visit with my parents. On the ride back to the parish, I regularly listened to the syndicated program *Power Line,* which was produced by the Southern Baptist Conference. This show intermingles gospel conversation with rock music. We developed a similar model, focusing our conversation on the Sunday readings.

Our show has been on many stations since its beginning in 1981. I usually wait for some station in the Chicago metropolitan area to undergo a programming change. In the midst of the chaos and confusion of the programming change, I approach the general manager with the possibility of the Catholic Church helping his or her new station through advertising the station in the many parishes in the archdiocese. The payoff for the Catholic Church, or in this case Holy Family Parish, is for us to have thirty minutes on the station. This formula of the church promoting the station and the station allowing the church to have time has been very successful. I am currently in the process of negotiating such an arrangement with a hard rock station that has gone oldies.

The culture of the radio industry has changed a great deal since 1981. In those days, religious programming was looked on as public service broadcasting that the station had to do. Since then, regulations have changed, lifting the requirement for public service. Often religious groups now have to pay a fee to get on the radio.

We currently are heard on WIND-AM, WCKG-FM, and WYLL-AM. As with all ministries at Holy Family, a Ministering Community has arisen for the production of the radio show. The radio show also has become part of an Internet radio service that we are providing called *The Stream,* taken from the notion of streaming via the Internet. A number of different programs play on *The Stream,* which people can connect with by computer.

I regularly close the radio broadcast by inviting those who do not have a church family to consider visiting Holy Family, or to consider worshiping with us. I tell them that the parish is a good parish, but we would be an even better parish if we had them with us. Note that part of our Communications subdivision's budget contains funds for radio production and broadcasting.

Some years ago, I learned that cable companies owed people in their neighborhoods cable access time for public service broadcasting. When that became evident to us, we began to think of broadcasting the radio show on TV, much as *Imus in the Morning* does on WFAN in New York City, and MSNBC on national cable. Our radio show is now seen in some sixty areas via the Comcast Cable Network in the Chicago metropolitan area. Our 9:00 a.m. Sunday Mass plays in about sixty neighborhoods via Comcast Cable.

We also began broadcasting a live audio version of our 7:30 a.m. Sunday Mass via the radio studio at Loyola University in Chicago, WLUW. This service is especially dedicated to people in Loyola Medical Center in Maywood, Ilinois. A videotaped version of our Sunday Mass also plays in about sixty neighborhoods at 1:00 p.m. on Sundays. We recently began iPod broadcasting and intend to do an audio version of the video transmissions of one of our weekly liturgies regularly on the Internet.

We have invested in technology that allows us to teleconference speakers, lecturers, and teachers from different parts of the metropolitan area, and the country, to our parish site. This has helped us to have speakers who either are too busy to travel, or are reluctant to travel, but who can get to a studio that can connect with our technology. One example of the use of this technology is that, over the years, we have offered master's-level courses here in our School of Ministry, with a teacher and some other students at Catholic Theological Union in Hyde Park teaching and seeing our parishioners and other students some fifty miles away in Inverness, Illinois. We now are planning such training with Loyola University Institute of Pastoral Ministry in Chicago.

Reaching Out

Before giving other examples of evangelizing through the media, let me clarify why we, and you, should use the media in this way. Often our evangelization efforts are "preaching to the choir." We are talking to the people who are connected with the parish, or invested in the church. It is important for us to reach out to the unchurched, the under-churched, those who are God- or community-deprived. We can do that through the media. Such media connection can lead to more in-depth relating to the parish.

One of our heart values as a parish is to tell the world around us about Jesus and about our faith community. We do not do this with arrogance, but we do do it with intentionality.

For some years we have also had a parish newspaper called *Connections*. *Connections* usually has a thematic article by staff members and myself, and announcements about upcoming events. We have distributed *Connections* in various ways: through bulk-mailings and the purchasing of mailing lists. We now drop *Connections* into sixty thousand *Chicago Tribunes* twice a year, on a Wednesday. We feel that this is an effective way of doing a kind of random reach-out to the northwest suburbs of Chicago. We also are negotiating to be part of *Faith* magazine, which will be sent to every registered parishioner.

Though we have not had the numerical success that a megachurch like Willow Creek has, we offer conferences here at Holy Family that other congregations and parishes are invited to. Once a year we have an Institute on Small Christian Communities, which surrounding parishes and Protestant congregations are invited to. We invited the entire metropolitan area to our conference on "The Purpose Driven Church," which we co-sponsored with Rick Warren's Saddleback organization. These conferences are other examples of reaching out to people. We regularly have had a Jesus Day, a ministry convention, at the parish on a Saturday in the fall. A group of parishioners have formed a Ministering Community to explore better uses of the Internet for evangelizing.

I ask every speaker who comes to Holy Family for permission to tape their presentation, and then we make their audiotape, videotape, or DVD available in our bookstore. Similarly, we audiotape the homily at every 9:00 a.m. Sunday Mass. They are on sale in the bookstore under the title *Homilies on Tape*.

The development of a bookstore has also been a communications effort to evangelize. We have in our bookstore Christian books, Christian music on tape and CD, and religious articles. Any books used in courses in our School of Ministry are likewise sold at the Holy Family Bookstore. The bookstore is run by a leader and co-leader, and a Ministering Community of parishioners.

Staying Connected

It became evident a few years ago that we were not marketing our services or ministries well. Attendance at talks, conferences, and events was not what it should or could have been. A number of us on staff began a search for a director of marketing. We found our first director of marketing in the person of Jim Accurso, who had experience in marketing on the international level for Motorola. The director of marketing's ministry is to help the ministries of Holy Family tell the world around us about Jesus and about Holy Family. Jim has gone to another job, but we are fine-tuning our understanding of and need for marketing as we look for a new director. New consultants are helping us understand the importance of branding for our market recognition purposes.

Through interactions with Tom Peters and his *Search for Excellence* materials, attendance at his Skunk Camp training program, and other research that I have done on the psychology of organizations, I have come to understand marketing in these terms: the work of marketing is to help people discover needs that they do not know yet that they have. The work of marketing is to turn boredom, ennui, lack of interest into curiosity, interest, desire, want, and "purchasing the product," or making a commitment to someone or an organization.

Many people in our culture are God-deprived and community-deprived. As the research mounts that parts of our brains are wired for God, spirituality, and prayer, as we discover anew that these realities make life better and more fruitful for people, we need to have strategies and ministers who will proactively reach out to people to remind them of their spiritual needs, and to remind them also that there is a faith community nearby that can help them with those needs. As the technology abounds and becomes more available, and more affordable, the opportunities to evangelize through the media and technology will also abound.

We are in the midst of a new capital campaign to help renovate our church and erect a new building, the Holy Family Center for Children, Youth, and Families. To help with the campaign, we have not produced a brochure, but rather have produced a DVD, hosted by many in leadership in the parish, that was given to every household in the parish. The DVD explained the nature of the campaign and solicited interest and support.

In a similar way, I do exegesis and hermeneutics for the fifteen hundred people in our Small Christian Communities on DVD. This DVD on the year-round Sunday readings is available to each leader of a Small Christian Community, either as a private resource or to play as part of the Small Christian Community meeting. For the groups that do the latter, this has been a way for me to stay connected with Small Christian Communities via technology, since I cannot be physically present to every group.

A local newspaper recently ran two articles that perhaps paint a portrait of what is going on in the world of evangelization. One of the lead stories on the front page was about eleven priests being defrocked because of sexual abuse in their past. The first page of the business section of that same newspaper carried the story that evangelical megachurches in the area, like Willow Creek and Harvest Bible Church, have grown 90 percent since 1980. The energy and creativity of the evangelical churches, and the inertia and pathology of the Catholic Church, was palpable. The Gospel that weekend was from Matthew, in which Jesus concluded with, "the Reign of God will be taken from you and given to those who will multiply its fruit." Catholic leaders, pay attention!

Chapter Six

Parish Governance

T HREE TIMES during my term at Holy Family, parish staff, leadership, and parishioners have articulated a parish vision, mission, and heart values.

I understand the vision of any organization as *who we are trying to be and become together.* An organization's mission is *the reason the organization exists.* Heart values, or principles, are *those values or convictions that prompt and motivate an organization and its personnel — what makes it tick.* In saying that we have articulated these three realities three times, what I really mean is that we have *fine-tuned them twice.* We really have not varied a great deal from the original version. What follows is the most recent version of these three statements:

Holy Family Vision

Holy Family Parish is a Catholic Christian community where all are welcome. By virtue of our baptism, we are sent to use our God-given gifts in service to God and others. We are called to evangelize and to witness God's love and mercy, to bring forgiveness and healing in a broken world, and to help people discern Christ's call to discipleship.

Holy Family Mission

Holy Family Parish exists to help with the emergence of the Reign of God by living the teachings of Jesus Christ. We continue the work of Jesus Christ, inviting all to understand his message of new life in the world. We strive to live the Reign of God. We share our faith in the domestic church of home, in small Christian communities, in our neighborhoods, and in the workplace.

Holy Family Principles and Heart Values

1. **Communication** of Jesus Christ and our faith community to the world around us.

2. **Evangelization** of all people toward conversion and life in God's Reign.

3. The **priesthood of the faithful** and **servant leadership** flowing from baptism, with empowerment through training and formation for ministry.

4. **Stewardship** of time, treasure, and gifts of the Holy Spirit.

5. Responsibility of all for **mercy, justice, and peace.**

6. **Small groups and basic Christian communities** as paradigmatic for our parish life.

7. The **domestic church** of home as the basic cell of church.

8. **Healing** a broken church and world through ministry, dialogue, prayer, forgiveness, and the celebration of the sacraments.

9. A community of lifelong **learners** committed to religious education from childhood through adulthood.

10. Embracing the **diversity** of all God's people.

Once an organization has articulated its vision, mission, and heart values, it must then find *structures that help it achieve these.* When I arrived at Holy Family there was really no governance system. There was an elected parish council, which worked pretty much in isolation from the ministries of the parish. In turn, the ministries operated in isolation, many with their own bank accounts and systems for making decisions. While I am sure some look back on those days of chaos as "the good old days," it was far from a collaborative, cooperative, discerning model.

After I became pastor, the parish council became increasingly aware of its ineffectiveness. Parish council leaders came to me, asking if we could explore a restructuring. In studying the restructuring of our parish council, we were led by the Spirit, I believe, to a very commonsense style of parish governance.

We researched many different models of parish councils. The one that made the most sense to us, at least in the mid 1990s, was called "the mini-council model." In this model, diverse areas of parish life, in a sense, have their own mini-parish council that makes decisions, sets direction, evaluates. Each mini-council selects one representative from that division of the parish who will serve on the Pastoral Council. Thus, governance, in effect, becomes a collaborative, cooperative *networking of the ministries.*

From my own experience at other parishes, I found the discernment of representatives at large to enrich the Pastoral Council. The model we came upon was that every other year the pastor would make recommendations of candidates at large, based on areas of parish need. Every alternate year, the existing Pastoral Council would give recommendations for candidates at large.

We originally had six areas of parish life that had mini-councils emerge within them: Evangelization and Catechesis; Operations; Pastoral Care; Outreach and Justice; Worship; and Family F.A.I.T.H. and Life.

No structure is an end in itself. Thus, our parish divisions have shifted over the years. In a renewed model, several years into the development of parish governance, the divisions became: Adult Formation; Family F.A.I.T.H. and Life; Worship; Operations; Outreach and Justice; Pastoral Care; Communications; and Youth Ministry.

Our latest configuration consists of eight leadership divisions:

- Adult Formation
- Evangelical Outreach
- Worship
- Family F.A.I.T.H. and Life
- Operations
- Pastoral Care
- Service, Justice and Peace
- Youth Ministry

With the initial six, now eight, leadership divisions, we have fashioned the mini-councils into what we call *Leadership Communities.* This was part of the whole paradigm shift toward community that we were experiencing with Small Christian Communities. Leadership Communities meet on the second Tuesday of each month at 7:00 p.m. They are made up of the leaders of the smallest units of ministry called *Ministering Communities.* Every Ministering Community finds its place under one of the eight umbrellas that we call Leadership Communities.

The role of the Leadership Community is to discern needs, do research, participate in pastoral planning, make decisions, provide education, and evaluate the work of a given division of ministry in the parish.

Allow me to share some insights regarding why the Leadership Communities' structure shifted. In the second redoing of the structure, Evangelization and Catechesis were separated out into Family F.A.I.T.H. and Life and Adult Formation, to give those ministries greater clarity, distinction, and direction. Youth Ministry was taken from the network of Evangelization and Catechesis ministries and was made a Leadership Community unto itself to better give the Youth Ministry position power, in the best sense of that term.

In the third redoing of the Leadership Communities, as we were preparing in our third pastoral plan, evangelization became a much more deliberate intention of both the archdiocese and the parish. A new Leadership Community was conceived entitled "Evangelical Outreach." This appropriated some of the Adult Formation ministries that had to do with initiation, ministry to the unchurched, and ministry to inactive Catholics, which became a unit under Evangelical Outreach entitled "Relational Ministries." The Communications division, largely having to do with print, TV, radio, and the Internet, became a subdivision of Evangelical Outreach entitled "Communications Ministries."

All the ministries under Evangelical Outreach proactively reach out to those on the margins of parish life or not included yet in parish life. This Leadership Community focuses on growth.

This is a portrait of what the Leadership Communities and the Ministering Communities look like. I also include the responsibilities and qualities of the leaders of Ministering Communities, Leadership Communities, and those that serve on the Pastoral Council.

Role of Ministering Communities

A. Ministering Communities coordinate all the activity of a given ministry.

B. Ministering Communities select a leader and co-leader for the ministry in consultation with the staff director/coordinator.

C. Ministering Communities' leaders and co-leaders serve an average of two years.

D. The leader of a Ministering Community also serves as a member of its relevant Leadership Community.

E. A Ministering Community works to assure:

   • Needs are listened to

   • Ministerial processes address each need

   • Gifts of the community are discerned and wedded to real needs

   • Yearly goals are set

   • Regular evaluation and reshaping of the ministry takes place relative to the goals

   • The basic laws governing human behavior — self-esteem, mutual respect, communication — are observed

   • The roles and tasks of a ministry are justly distributed to all members

F. A Ministering Community ought to have a Mission Statement that articulates the ministry's mission, in cooperation with the larger mission of the parish.

G. A Ministering Community makes sure all of its members are empowered.

H. A Ministering Community makes sure all of its members are adequately formed and trained.

I. A Ministering Community grounds its activities in the rich soil of prayer, scripture, and life sharing.

J. A Ministering Community lives out its collaborative connection to other Ministering Communities, Leadership Communities, the Pastoral Council, the pastoral staff, and the parish at large.

Role of Leadership Communities

A. To bring together representative leaders of ministries in the community to develop a wholistic approach to a given area of ministry.

B. To foster community among leaders.

C. To develop vision for areas of parish ministry.

D. To engage in long- and short-range planning and goal setting.

E. To engage in ongoing evaluation and reshaping of ministry efforts.

F. To select from membership a representative to the Pastoral Council.

G. To provide faith formation for ministry leaders.

H. To provide training for ministry leaders.

I. To provide a healthy balance at meetings for business, formation, and training.

J. To provide an environment of prayer, scripture sharing, and life sharing for those leading in ministry.

The Work of a Pastoral Council

A. To harness leaders of parish ministries, groups and communities, and representatives-at-large in a synergistic effort at vision, long- and short-range planning, and evaluation of parish efforts.

B. To work collaboratively with the parish staff in accomplishing parish pastoral direction as it is cooperatively discerned.

C. To unite the work of staff, Leadership Communities, and Ministering Communities toward a greater spirit and behavior of collaboration.

D. To work with the pastor and pastoral staff in both studying and discerning the future direction for parish life.

E. To work with the pastor and pastoral staff in shaping and reshaping parish structures to better facilitate a mission of evangelization and emergence of the Reign of God.

F. To work cooperatively and collaboratively with all parish organizations in incarnating the parish heart values of stewardship, evangelization, baptismal ministry, community (including family consciousness), and collaboration.

G. To work with the pastor, pastoral staff, and all other parish organisms toward the felt experience of unity in its mission, which is church.

H. To work with the pastor, pastoral staff, and all other organisms toward connection and interdependence with the Archdiocese of Chicago, the universal church, and other pastoral alliances with other faith communities or parishes.

I. To engage in the ministry of leadership for the entire parish.

J. To ensure a healthy balance in its agenda of:

- Shared prayer
- Reflection on scripture
- Life sharing
- Ministry and business

The Ministering Community is the basic unit of ministry. We encourage each ministry to have a leader, a co-leader, and a Ministering Community. Ministering Communities meet according to their own timetable and strategies. Some meet monthly. Some meet quarterly. They must meet at least quarterly to have an identity.

The position of the co-leader, in addition to being an active person in the ministry, is to serve as an *apprentice,* ready to take over the position of leadership in two or three years. We encourage leaders to think in terms of their leadership as that of *two or three years.*

Each Ministering Community is to spend the first twenty minutes of its meetings, whenever, however they meet, in Faith First. Faith First is that mini-experience of a Small Christian Community involving the proclamation of next Sunday's Gospel, the sharing of one of the *Sharing Faith* booklet's faith-sharing questions, petitions, and the Lord's Prayer. As I mentioned before, having all the ministries do Faith First has dramatically changed the quality of Ministering Communities' meetings, as well as enriched the celebration of the weekend Eucharist, with so many people having attended to the Word before they come to church.

All of the Ministering Communities within a given division select a leader and a co-leader for the Leadership Community that they are part of. Thus, some people find themselves to be both the leader of a Ministering Community and the leader or co-leader of a Leadership Community.

All of our Leadership Communities meet on the second Tuesday of the month at 7:00 p.m. The first experience is a communal experience of Faith First, with each of the eight Leadership Communities doing faith sharing and prayer within their own group. Then, the focus of each of the Tuesday meetings alternates between faith formation, ministerial training, and business. On many of the second Tuesday evenings, at least some time must be given to business within each unique Leadership Community. Some nights (for example, evenings on budgeting, goal setting, evaluation) the whole evening is given to business.

Ministerial training of all eight of the Leadership Communities focuses on topics that leaders need to grow in: how to set goals and objectives; how to run an effective meeting; the twelve disciplines of an empowerment approach to ministry (which will be covered in another chapter); empowerment and animation; the meaning of ministry. A whole year was spent simply on the significant evangelization documents that have been produced by our church over the past thirty years. Each Leadership Community contributed practical suggestions for our pastoral plan for 2005–2010, *New Image of Parish (Revised),* which has a decided evangelization focus (see the appendix, page 143, for the entire plan).

More than any other experience I have had in parish life, Leadership Community meetings, while chaotic at times, have brought various ministries into meaningful collaboration, cooperation, and communication with each other.

At the very outset when we began Leadership Community meetings, some ministries that were accustomed to working in isolation resisted attendance and involvement. We gently had to communicate to them that this is how we are doing parish governance now and in the future, and if they wanted to continue in ministry, they would have to adapt to the common disciplines the rest of the parish was committing to.

The Parish Pastoral Council

The generation of our eight mini-councils, or Leadership Communities, eventually led to the emergence of our Pastoral Council. Each Leadership Community selects a member to be the representative of that division of parish life. Those eight members are foundational to the council. The discernment process takes place at parish Leadership Community meetings when given council candidates' terms are up. All terms are staggered so as to provide a healthy continuity and rotation of members. The discernment process begins months before the actual evening of discernment. From each Leadership Community, names are generated and candidates are asked about their willingness to serve. At the Leadership Community, when the actual decision is made as to who should go to council, each proposed candidate is discussed thoroughly by the given Leadership Community. The discussion is contextualized by prayer. Then each Leadership Community member is polled as to which candidate the Holy Spirit is prompting him or her to decide upon. The discussion continues until there is a consensus on the candidate for council. A similar prayerful process is engaged in for every decision that the council makes, as well as all decisions made by Leadership Communities.

We also decided that it was very important not just to have an adult representative for Youth Ministry, but also a teen, and so we ask our Youth Ministry Leadership Community also to select a high-school student who, with the adult selected by the Youth Ministry Leadership Community, represents parish youth on the Pastoral Council.

For the last several years, the outgoing chairperson of the Pastoral Council has become the representative to the archdiocesan Pastoral Council. That person also serves as a kind of emeritus figure serving on the Pastoral Council, which he or she formerly led, representing the archdiocese.

Every year there is a discernment process to select a chairperson for the Pastoral Council, as well as a co-chairperson. While the chairperson is the dominant figure of the two in terms of leadership, we encourage the co-chairperson to see himself or herself as *apprenticing* to become the next chairperson. With only one exception, the co-chairperson has been selected to be the next chairperson of the Pastoral Council.

Finally, in terms of membership, a representative of the parish staff is selected to sit on the council. For example, the current staff member representing the parish staff on Pastoral Council is Dawn Mayer, pastoral associate, director of Family F.A.I.T.H. and Life, and director of pastoral ministry. Thus, fifteen members constitute the council. It is a large council, but not unwieldy.

The Pastoral Council meets on the third Tuesday of the month from 7:00 p.m. to 9:30 p.m. Meetings begin with Faith First, that mini-experience of a Small Christian Community that is part of all parish meetings. This lasts approximately twenty minutes with a rotation on the part of council members for leadership of that segment.

In the business part of the meeting, which comes first, attention is given to new initiatives or proposals, or updates on past decisions or projects. It has been our experience that new initiatives or proposals can start anyplace in the parish system. The proposal can come from parish staff, Ministering Communities, Leadership Communities, parishioners at large, or the council.

THE QUALITIES OF THE THREE COMMUNITIES' LEADERS

Ministering Community Leader	Leadership Community Leader	Pastoral Council Leader

Vision:
   Understanding
   Commitment
	Vision:
	   Understanding
	   Commitment
		Vision:
		   Understanding
		   Commitment

Community builder	Focused	**Big picture**
Good listener	Seeker/Evaluator	Humble servant
Able to communicate	Provides direction and guidance	Maturity
Empowers	**Wider/deeper understanding of ministry(ies)**	**Effective communicator**
Knows the work of the ministry	Understands/executes good training	Skilled at discernment
Support/Mentor	Forward thinking/visionary	Confident in his/her being chosen
Responsible follow-through	Open to diverse opinions	Forward thinking/visionary
Organized	**Ability to suspend personal agenda**	Seasoned in ministry
Conflict management	Respect for larger church	**Consensus builder**
People skills	**Collaborative**	Available and accessible
Network with others	Models and facilitates prayer	**Time**
Balanced and boundaries	**Willingness to spend extra time**	Team player
Contagious enthusiasm (faith-ministry)		**Reflector and synthesizer**
Implements small groups		Respects all people/roles
Adaptable		Inclusive
Grounded in mission		
Sees life/faith connection		

THE TASKS OF THE THREE COMMUNITIES' LEADERS

Ministering Community Leader	Leadership Community Leader	Pastoral Council Leader
To work with professional staff member(s) and the Ministering Community in planning specifics of a given ministry	To work with professional staff members and leaders of Ministering Communities in harnessing the Ministering Communities in a given area of parish life toward a common vision of the ministry	To represent a given area of ministry to the Pastoral Council
To work collaboratively also evaluating a given ministry	To work collaboratively with the above personnel in naming goals and doing long-range planning for a given area of parish life	To work collaboratively with other council leaders in long-range planning for the parish at large as well as evaluation and reshaping of parish-wide efforts
To care for the administration of the ministry in cooperation with professional staff member(s) and the leader of the relevant Leadership Community	To work collaboratively also in the evaluation and reshaping of a given area of parish life	To work collaboratively with the pastor, pastoral professional staff, and Leadership and Ministering Communities toward the achievement of short- and long-range plans for the parish
To empower all who are part of the ministry to use their gifts of the Holy Spirit to fulfill the mission of the ministry	To work collaboratively in achieving a healthy balance, at community meetings of business, training, and faith formation	To advise the pastor on current and future directions for the parish
	To lead the ministries represented within a Leadership Community toward excellence in servant leadership	To work with the above personnel in advancing the parish heart values of stewardship, ministry, and collaboration
		To work collaboratively to ensure that parish structures advance the mission of the Reign of God and conversion

For a new initiative to be acted on, it must be evaluated by all organisms that are involved: pastoral staff, the given Ministering Community and Leadership Community that will be involved in the effort. All initiatives must pass through the discernment of the Pastoral Council to become a parish initiative.

After dealing with proposals and reports, each Leadership Community representative is given time to report on what is going on in his or her Leadership Community. I give a pastor's report. Dawn Mayer gives a report on the staff.

Council sessions are open to the public. There are times when the council has closed sessions, or sessions that at least in part are closed, because of highly sensitive or highly charged issues that are being talked about and are not ready to be presented to the parish at large.

It has been my experience that Pastoral Council members take their work very seriously. Though by archdiocesan policy they are advisory in nature, my approach to them has been to relate to them as if they were extended staff. No major initiative may take place in the parish without the council's discernment and decision for it.

About a year and a half ago the Worship Leadership Community proposed renovations for our worship space, which was getting close to twenty years old. I proposed the research on and eventual action on the construction of a religious education center to create a better environment for Holy Family Catholic Academy (our parish school), Family F.A.I.T.H. gatherings (our religious education effort for families of children in public schools), and junior high and high-school Youth Ministry.

The council appointed a space analysis subgroup to study how we are using current space, and to study also the goals and objectives of our Pastoral Plan for the next five years and to determine what kind of space would be needed to implement these goals and objectives. The space committee recommended the construction of new space. This committee then began to work with an architectural firm and a construction firm to create both what the renovated worship space and what a new religious education center might look like. Various models were generated as well as costs for each model. After studying the models for three meetings, as well as engaging in a number of focus group meetings with parishioners at large and a town hall meeting on the issue of liturgical renovation and new construction, the council finally decided, after a year and a half of work, to move on liturgical renovations and to begin the fundraising needed to construct the new religious education center and the liturgical renovations.

The council studied past financial campaigns in the parish and discovered that the parish usually raised around $6 million. It was the recommendation of the Pastoral Council that the Building Ministering Community begin to shape up plans for a building that would cost approximately $6 million, and plans also for liturgical renovation in the neighborhood of $1 million. This is a recent example of how decisions are reached at Holy Family Parish.

Another example of how decisions are made through parish governance occurred recently with regard to a newly proposed Thomas Ministry. A wife and mother, concerned about struggling with religious and spiritual doubt in her husband and adolescent son, came to me to propose a new ministry that would serve those in painful, doubting periods regarding God and faith. I endorsed the idea. She proposed that it be done on two tracks: one for teens, and one for adults. I recommended that she bring her proposal to the Evangelical Outreach Leadership Community the following Tuesday evening. Should the Leadership Community react positively, their representative to the Pastoral Council would then bring it to the council. I, in turn, would bring it back to staff directors. Hopefully there would be consensus on such a new ministry by staff, Leadership Community, and Pastoral Council. The next challenge then is to begin to develop the ministry, seeking parishioners to be the Ministering Community, and from the emerging Ministering Community, a needed leader and co-leader.

Such a process approach to decision making certainly slows things down in terms of making decisions and taking action, but it has also been our experience that the process assures greater "buy in" by many constituents rather than a few people doing their self-ordained own thing. For example, there was quite divided opinion about the construction of a religious education center. Three or four months before the last Pastoral Council meeting where consensus was reached that we should move ahead on the fundraising and planning for construction, several people on the council experienced a genuine metanoia, or change of mind and heart, regarding the need for an improved environment for religious education for our children and teens.

The council has retreat days on a regular basis. These are planned by subgroups of the council and myself and/or the staff member on council. These retreat days, usually on a Saturday, end with the council going to the Saturday afternoon Mass followed by a dinner to which council members' families are invited. The inclusion of family members at the end of the day is an attempt at family consciousness, a principle to which the parish is committed.

Chapter Seven

Empowerment for Ministry

O NE OF THE INGREDIENTS in the movement from good to great in Jim Collins's book *Good to Great* is the development of *a culture of discipline*. A culture of discipline speaks of shared values, convictions, and behaviors that all in an organization are committed to. One of the areas of parish life where a culture of discipline has been most evident at Holy Family is in empowering the baptized for ministry.

Let me begin this chapter by sharing an explanation of ministry as it is experienced at Holy Family. Some of this is borrowed from Thomas O'Meara's *Theology of Ministry*; some is my own emphasis. *Ministry is being or doing by a baptized follower of Jesus using gifts of the Holy Spirit, present in every person, to help with the emergence of the Reign of God in a community, institution, workplace, society, or the world in general.* Let's tease out some of the key elements in this explanation.

Sometimes ministry involves just *being* who we are for and with another person or other people. In this being who we are, we can give witness to the power and presence of God alive within us. In being who we are, through our values and convictions, we can transform the world around us toward the vision of Jesus Christ. Ministry is most often *doing*. It is behavior. It is behavior with, for, and toward others.

Baptism is the font from which ministry flows. Holy Orders has to do with a special kind of ministry, but ministry in general finds its origins in our baptism. Through baptism we are called to be servant leaders in imitation of Jesus.

Ministry involves the use of *gifts*. The baptized are all charismatic people, gifted with the very power of God, the power of the Holy

Spirit. Over the years, working with the North American Forum on the Catechumenate, presenting institutes and seminars around the world, and certainly working in the parish as pastor, I have distinguished different kinds of gifts.

There are *gifts of being,* gifts that are at the very core of who we are as persons. Gifts of being involve our emotional patterns, our cognitive patterns, our behavioral patterns, our values, our convictions, our personalities and personality types, our temperaments. Gifts of being also include the mystery of suffering in our lives, the time we have spent with Jesus in the mystery of the cross.

Gifts of doing are abilities that each person has based on natural or acquired talents. Gifts of doing refer to what a person does well. These gifts may be connected to one's life work, hobbies, or passions.

I also speak of *the classical gifts of the Holy Spirit.* Though the gifts of the Spirit are mentioned many places in scripture, there are several passages that I think are most helpful and instructive. The first is Isaiah 11:1–4. Others from the New Testament are 1 Corinthians 12:1–31, 1 Corinthians 13:1–13, and 1 Corinthians 14:1–40. Another succinct passage is 1 Peter 4:10–11.

Our faith community believes that all the baptized are blessed with gifts, yet seldom have baptized Christians been helped to reflect on their giftedness. We have a ministry at Holy Family entitled "Gifted," which I will explain more in depth later, the specific purpose of which is to help people discern giftedness. As the ministry has developed, it has helped people to reflect not only on parish or ecclesial ministries, but also on their giftedness and their motivation for their work in the world.

The goal of ministry is to help with *the emergence of God's Reign.* All ministry is focused on God's Reign. We can see here the convergence of ministry and evangelization. As evangelization is all about inviting people to conversion and the Reign of God, ministry has the same goal. *All ministry should be evangelizing.*

The Reign of God does not happen in a vacuum. It needs to be incarnated, enfleshed. Many of us try to make the Reign of God happen in and through our parishes. For others, the Reign of God emerges in hospitals, institutions of healing, schools. Ultimately ministry is an attempt to transform society and the world into what Jesus meant by the Reign of God. Thus, evangelization and ministry are never retreats from the world, but movement toward, and the transformation of, the world.

Lateral Ministry

For almost thirty years I have been influenced by a vision of ministry that developed at an organization called the Center for Pastoral Ministry in the Archdiocese of Chicago. The Center for Pastoral Ministry, which later became the Center for Ministry Development, cooperated with the University of St. Mary of the Lake/Mundelein Seminary to begin a doctor of ministry program. In the mid-1970s I was part of the first D.Min. class. Three pioneers in the development of ministry were Dr. John Shea, Dr. Gerard Egan, and the late Fr. Larry Gorman, a priest of the Archdiocese of Chicago. They spoke of *lateral ministry,* comparing it to *vertical ministry.*

Vertical ministry is the old hierarchical/clerical model of ministry. In this model, a trained or educated person directly delivers ministerial services to a target population.

Lateral ministry refers to an empowerment model of ministry. In this approach, the trained or educated person does not vertically hand down ministerial services, but rather spends significant time raising up ministry leaders who will work, using the language of Holy Family, with a Ministering Community to focus on a given target population. Staff train and form leaders who in turn empower Ministering Communities, which serve specific target populations.

All the professional ministerial staff at Holy Family were hired, are supervised, and are evaluated on their ability to do lateral, or empowerment-style, ministry. Sometimes it would be easier for ministry directors, associate directors, or coordinators (our professional staff) to do things by themselves. Ministry will always necessitate that we do some direct delivery of service to parishioners. For those of us who are in professional ministry, if we did not do some direct delivery of services, we would dry up inside. But a significant amount of our staff's time is spent not doing *for,* but doing *with* — training, empowering, and learning with the leaders and ministers who are being empowered.

There are now 150 ministries at Holy Family. In the ideal order, each ministry is to have a leader and a co-leader. The co-leader shares in some of the leadership tasks with the leader and is also apprenticing to take over leadership in two or three years. The role of the co-leader is vital. Without a co-leader, if the leader has to leave the ministry, the ministry can easily go into a tailspin. Thus, at least two persons in leadership are vital for each Ministering Community.

Each Ministering Community is made up of a variety of people using their gifts for a unique ministerial focus or task. The empowerment model that I have included here should be the discipline of every ministry. I train staff leaders to give ministry away. I tell them, "You should be able to leave your position and the ministry would continue to flourish." Any good staff member is raising up, training and forming, empowering and enabling parishioners to own and carry out parish ministry. Good staff members do not take the ministry with them if they leave the parish.

This understanding of ministry sometimes creates a bit of a job threat in staff members, but it need not. There are enough pastoral needs and work in a parish community to keep all of us in professional ministry sufficiently busy. Once a ministry is made strong it frees staff members to look at other areas of ministry that need development.

Staff members ought to be *empowering consultants,* and despite how strong ministry leaders and a Ministering Community might become, these empowering consultants are responsible for staying connected with each ministry they are responsible for. No ministry is to "do its own thing."

We do not speak the language of "teams" and "boards" at Holy Family. A Ministering Community is part of the paradigm shift that has been gong on for ten years. The 150 Ministering Communities are task-oriented. Nonetheless, whenever the ministry meets, fifteen or twenty minutes are given to the Faith First experience. Proclamation of next weekend's Gospel, discussion of several faith-sharing questions, petitions, and a closing prayer precede any business at a Ministering Community or Leadership Community gathering. I want to emphasize that Faith First has dramatically changed the tone of our parish.

The Disciplines

There are twelve disciplines that we live out of in this empowerment model:

1. Discernment of Needs

Too often in ministry we ascribe needs to people rather than listening for needs and trying to respond. Each Leadership Community and each Ministering Community is challenged to listen for the needs of their focus group. Programming then is determined by needs.

2. Statement of Vision and Mission

As I have already mentioned, an organization's vision statement is an articulation of *who* or *what* a group of people is trying to be together. A mission statement states *why* they exist as a group. Realizing that the parish has an overall vision and mission statement, each Ministering Community and each Leadership Community articulates its vision and mission in relation to the greater vision and mission of the parish.

3. Articulation of Heart Values and Principles

The articulation of heart values and principles is done by the parish at large. It needs to be done also on the level of Leadership Communities and Ministering Communities. Thus, each organism within the larger organism of the parish is purpose driven. Each Small Christian Community also has a covenant prayer that articulates each Small Christian Community's mission. Heart values and principles refer to the convictions that make an organization tick and enliven the organization. Heart values and principles refer to the passion of the organization.

4. Goals and Objectives

Goals refer to the broad, overarching aims of an organization. Objectives are clear, manageable, measurable steps toward the goals. Goals and objectives for Leadership Communities and Ministering Communities flow from ongoing need discernment and study of the current parish plan. The current articulation of our parish plan is entitled *New Image of Parish (Revised).*

5. Discernment of Gifts

Each ministry should help its members discern their giftedness. The "Gifted" process, which I will speak of later and which we have employed for close to ten years in our parish, includes steps that can easily be adapted for use in each ministry.

6. Deciding on Roles

A kind of nouveau clericalism can creep into lay ministry. People can enjoy too much the gratification that ministry brings and begin to become ministerial gluttons, trying to do too much ministry by themselves. Flowing from discernment of gifts should be a discernment of roles — *who* will do *what* in the ministry.

7. Distribution of Tasks

Tasks are distributed in a Ministering Community and a Leadership Community based on gifts and roles. For example, in Neighborhood Ministry there are three main functions: connecting with neighbors, inviting neighbors to social events, and inviting neighbors to home-based worship and liturgies. In the Core Community for Neighborhood Ministry, leadership ought to be provided to neighborhood ministers for these three challenges. People gifted in each *unique* part of Neighborhood Ministry should be empowered to help others. No one person has to take on the responsibility of overseeing all three areas of responsibility.

8. Time-Lining

Goals and objectives should be rolled out in an ordered sort of way based on a gradual unfolding in time. Where does the organization want to be in three months, six months, nine months, one year?

9. Communication

It is always surprising how people or organizations think that they are communicating when, in fact, they are communicating incompletely or not at all. Our banner slogan is "You cannot communicate enough." Information is power. Needed information in a ministry needs to be clearly, regularly shared with anyone involved in the ministry. Hidden agendas, private logic, and ministerial cliques are not helpful. In addition to information, feelings and convictions should also be communicated, when appropriate.

10. Climate Control

Abraham Maslow said years ago that people want to go only where they feel they are wanted and welcomed, where they can feel self-esteem. The leader of a Ministering Community, the leader of a Leadership Community, the leader of a Small Christian Community or any organism functioning in a parish, needs to make sure that the relational climate is *nurturing, welcoming, helping people to feel that they are making an important contribution in some area of parish life.*

11. Evaluation

Parish ministries at Holy Family regularly evaluate themselves according to the goals and objectives they have set for a given year. On the following page is a form we used for an exercise at a recent Leadership Community meeting.

12. Learning and Reshaping

There is no such thing as failure in evangelization and ministry. Rather, the approach we should take is that of learning and reshaping. What worked? What did not work? Let's try again! But in trying again, how should we tweak our efforts to ensure greater effectiveness?

PASTORAL REPORT

Name of Leadership Community _____

Name of Staff Director _____

Name of Leader and Co-Leader _____

_____

1. What were the goals and objectives of your Leadership Community for 2004/2005?

2. How would you evaluate achievement of the goals and objectives that you set for 2004/2005?

3. What are the goals and objectives for your Leadership Community for 2005/2006?

Discerning Gifts

A central part of our Gifted process is teaching parishioners the steps and skills of discernment. The root meaning of the Latin infinitive *discernere* means to sift through or sort through. As followers of Jesus, we should be doing discernment in several different ways. Disciples should take moral discernment seriously, judging right and wrong, good and evil, what is just and unjust. In empowering parishioners for ministry, discernment of gifts is a necessary discipline.

What are the steps of discernment? Whatever the direction of discernment, in my experience, the steps are as follows:

- Pray to the Holy Spirit for wisdom and guidance throughout the process.

- In a spirit of what Carl Rogers called congruence, listen to yourself, listen within, and name what you find in your own self-listening.

- Go to others for affirmation, challenge, or expansion of what you have discovered.

- Continue to pray.

- Evaluate options.

- Generate possibilities.

- Make a decision.

- Take action.

- Evaluate your decision and action.

- Reshape your efforts, if necessary.

In applying these steps to the discernment of gifts, one ought to engage in activities like these:

- Pray for the guidance of the Holy Spirit.

- Listen within to what might be your gifts of being. Gifts of being refer to those abilities that lie at the core of a person's self or personality. They include personality type, character, values, passions, conversion experiences, and experiences of the mystery of the cross.

◆ Listen for what might be your gifts of doing. Gifts of doing refer to abilities that a person has in performance. Often these are related to professional skills or to skills acquired through hobbies or personal interests.

◆ Listen to how you may share in the classical gifts of the Holy Spirit, spoken of earlier in the scripture passages that I highlighted.

◆ Go to others for affirmation, challenge, or expansion.

How would we join our discerned gifts of being and doing and the classical gifts of the Spirit as found in scripture to the needs of the parish? Through a similar process, the discerning person needs to listen to the needs of the parish.

We expose people to our pastoral needs by walking them through our eight divisions of parish ministry: Adult Faith Formation; Evangelical Outreach; Family F.A.I.T.H. and Life; Operations; Service, Justice and Peace; Pastoral Care; Worship; and Youth Ministry. We do this through ministry fairs held in the large narthex of our church and through printed material that we distribute at church.

In discerning a ministry, we ask parishioners to listen deeply to the self; to discern what gifts one has and what ministries seem to fit one's gifts; to go to others for affirmation, challenge, and expansion; and then to generate possibilities, make a decision, evaluate as one gets into the ministry, and reshape ministerial efforts, if that is needed.

The Gifted process at Holy Family has been experienced in recent years in many different ways. It has been packaged as a workshop, taking place on several evenings. It has been offered on weekends as a one-day workshop. Materials have been prepared to work on at home. Materials are distributed at our welcoming of newcomers sessions. Materials have been distributed at our new Mini-Retreat 101 model on faith, membership, and stewardship. This year we began offering Gifted workshops or "labs" throughout the year for parishioners who are not only looking at ecclesial ministries, but also in general want to spend time prayerfully looking at their gifts and the needs around them.

We just completed a Gifted process that began on Pentecost Sunday. Parishioners were given several weeks after Pentecost to spend time, especially as families, choosing ministries that individuals or the family could become involved in. As of this writing, 330 commitment forms have been turned in, with some people choosing more than one ministry.

We took a big step forward in a recent Gifted process in producing the booklet *Your Talents, Your Community, Your Voice.* Each of our parish ministries is described under one of the eight divisions of ministry. As I mentioned earlier, next to the description of the ministry are listed the gifts of being that might be utilized in that ministry, as well as the gifts of doing, and the contact person and his or her phone number and e-mail address, so that parishioners can easily connect with a leader of a ministry if they are so interested. We want to expand on this information in future editions of this booklet to include other information that would better help people make a decision about their involvement.

While offering people opportunities to discern their gifts is important, it is also important to offer training and formation for ministry if people are to be truly empowered. As mentioned earlier, we now have a School of Ministry that involves the Gifted process, the CALLED two-year leadership certificate, certificates in Parish Life and Administration and Spiritual Companioning, BA-level courses, as well as MA-level courses. College credits are offered in conjunction with the pastoral ministry departments of local universities.

Over the years we have learned that we probably cared better for new ministers than we did for experienced ministers. Thus, several years ago we tried to break out of the syndrome of training new ministers and then letting them go their own way. We have tried rather to add other opportunities for ongoing training of ministers after they have been in ministry for some time, to be renewed in spirituality, theology, and skills for ministry.

The June 19, 2006, edition of *U.S. News & World Report* contained an interesting article by David Gergen entitled "Bad News for Bullies." The notion of servant leadership, as lived by Jesus Christ and taught by Robert Greenleaf, was discussed. Greenleaf was quoted as saying, "A new moral principle is emerging in which followers will respond only to individuals who are chosen as leaders because they are proven and trusted as servants." Gergen goes on to say that "increasingly the best leaders are those who don't order, but persuade; don't dictate, but draw out; don't squeeze, but grow the people around them. They push power out of the front office down into the organization, and become a leader of leaders.... At a time when young professionals are looking for a different set of values and work, studies show they are less interested in power and prestige than in positive relations with colleagues and interesting challenges." What Gergen describes in his article is what we seek to achieve in ministry training and formation at Holy Family Parish.

Chapter Eight

Mercy and Justice

I N THAT GREAT BLUEPRINT for Catholic evangelization, the apostolic exhortation *Evangelii Nuntiandi*, Paul VI in 1975 reminded us that the work of evangelization is incomplete if proclamation and witnessing and programs are not joined also to the work of mercy, justice, and liberation. So also, the mission of a parish is incomplete if the parish is not intentional about the works of mercy and justice. If we just look to the example of Jesus, the work of the Reign of God involved his teaching and bringing meaning into peoples lives, but the teaching always led to healing and liberation from constricting forces that robbed people of their human dignity. The parish, in imitation of Jesus, must make part of its mission mercy and justice.

When I speak of actions of mercy and ministries of mercy, I am speaking of charity, of parishioners in diverse ways sharing their resources with those less fortunate than they.

The work of justice is different. At Holy Family we have distinguished three classical understandings of justice. There is *commutative justice,* in which we strive as disciples to be just, honest, and truthful in all of our ways, all of our dealings with our fellow human beings. There is *distributive justice,* which seeks to insure that the world's resources are shared, distributed among all of God's people around the world. The gap between rich and poor is widening. Very few people around the world control very much of the wealth of the world, while so many others struggle in conditions of homelessness, poverty, and hunger. Obviously parishes should be about the work of both commutative and distributive justice.

Social justice involves confrontation with societal, cultural systems that dehumanize people, rob them of their freedom, their rights, and their dignity. We often talk a lot about social justice in Catholic environments, but we do not often get to the work of social justice in practical, ministerial ways.

One of the eight divisions of Holy Family's governance structure is the ministries under the umbrella of "Service, Justice and Peace." Each of these ministries is constituted as a Ministering Community, with a leader, co-leader, and Ministering Community. The ministries are taught, trained, and encouraged to use the skills of empowerment and discernment of gifts in actualizing their ministries. All of these Ministering Communities, in turn, are represented in the Service, Justice and Peace Leadership Community. The Service, Justice and Peace Leadership Community also selects a representative to the Pastoral Council.

Over the years, parish staff and leadership have articulated broad goals for our mercy-justice involvement. They are:

1. advocating the *seamless garment* vision of respect for life;

2. confronting homelessness, hunger, and poverty;

3. working toward an end to capital punishment;

4. supporting education for economically challenged young people;

5. supporting some international ministries of mercy and justice, economically and through presence and involvement;

6. upholding the dignity of work and the worker;

7. caring for creation and ecological concerns.

For the next several years, the Service, Justice and Peace Leadership Community will address each of these seven concerns with the methodology suggested by Paul VI in *A Call to Action* (1971): prayer; discernment and study; a practical action plan for each of the seven.

Most of the ministries contained within the Service, Justice and Peace Leadership Community are ministries of mercy. I will describe later a long-term, broad-based justice ministry that we share with a community organization in the area of our parish. The ministries within Service, Justice and Peace are as follows:

- *Assist-A-Family* — This ministry matches parish donor families, work groups, and Small Christian Communities confidentially with community and parish families in need for four holidays a year: Easter, Labor Day/Back to School, Thanksgiving, and Christmas. A full meal is provided, as well as gifts appropriate for the holiday.

- *Clothing Drives* are conducted twice yearly for the benefit of the needy and homeless near the St. Vincent de Paul Center in Chicago.

- *The Holy Family Food Pantry* distributes quality food throughout the year to needy families and individuals and sponsors parish-wide food drives as needed.

- *Hispanic Ministry* recognizes the need to foster a relationship with the local Hispanic community. Support and resources are offered to meet the needs of that community.

- *Holiday Sharing* organizes and coordinates parish-wide Christmas and Easter gifts to benefit needy individuals in the Chicago-land area.

- *Individual Needs* assesses individual, confidential requests for financial assistance and other help, and directs people to specific programs or community agencies as emergency needs arise.

- *Misión Juan Diego* is a Hispanic mission church near our parish. Our parish works with the mission in assisting economically disadvantaged Hispanics.

- *Peace and Justice* is a cluster of six suburban churches in the area joining forces to create just and peaceful communities. Affordable housing, mentoring to local needy families through Catholic churches, and supporting peace efforts are a few of the issues being addressed.

- *Preservation of Human Dignity (PHD)* is a not-for-profit, respect life volunteer organization offering women's counseling at a center located in nearby Palatine. PHD counsels women to enlighten them to the alternatives to abortion. PHD is not a radical anti-abortion organization. It truly understands the needs of women at a time when they are faced with the most difficult of decisions. PHD is an independent organization that Holy Family both supports and collaborates with.

◆ *Prison Ministry* provides outreach to prisoners and their families in Lake, Cook, and McHenry counties.

◆ *Public Action to Deliver Shelter (PADS)* is a program of emergency help for the homeless. PADS provides services at several suburban churches from October to April. We are one of those churches. Hot food is provided to participants from 7:00 to 8:30 p.m. Guests then sleep on a four-inch foam mattress with sheets, a blanket, and a pillow. Separate areas are provided for women, men, and families. Holy Family is a host site on Sunday evenings. Other local churches take care of other nights.

◆ *Respect Life* educates and helps parishioners individually and collectively to form a consistent ethic of life (seamless garment) on issues from womb to tomb.

◆ *St. Joseph Home for the Elderly* is a not-for-profit home for the elderly near Holy Family Parish. The elderly ministered to are economically disadvantaged. The home is operated by the Little Sisters of the Poor, and the parish supports the work of the home in a variety of ways.

◆ *St. Michael the Archangel Parish* on the southeast side of the city is a sharing parish for Holy Family. We seek to serve the poor and the homeless through a soup kitchen, a pantry, and aiding St. Michael's school.

◆ *The Social Justice Network* maintains a room at Holy Family called the Social Justice Room. Reading materials and information on projects for justice and mercy are available in this room. It resembles a reading room, with additional audiovisual materials.

◆ *Faith That Does Justice* and *Salt and Light* are educational processes about and involvement in justice work. I will say more about these later.

- *WINGS (Women In Need Growing Stronger)* is an organization for women and children who are victims of domestic violence. Holy Family helps with housing, job skills, and various other needs.

- *The Pathway Development Institute* works with a local community center, Journey From PADS to Hope. This project focuses on the needs of the homeless by providing qualified candidates with individual counseling, training and mentoring, increasing levels of responsibility, independence and trust in a secure twenty-four-hour safe and nurturing environment. The program will provide different levels of housing for people, from a PADS site (food and overnight shelter) in one part of the building, to dormitory living in another part of the building, to independent apartment living in another part of the building. In addition to this temporary housing education, counseling, training in job skills will also be provided. The ultimate goal of the ministry is a graduation to employment and independent living. We currently are in search of a site for the building and a director.

In starting both PADS and the Pathway Development Institute we have run into "spatial racism" on the part of neighbors close to the parish and among our own parishioners. By spatial racism I mean there are some people who are intellectually open to the mercy and justice work we are about in the parish, but they do not want us to do this work in the parish or in the neighborhood. This has necessitated some education of our own parishioners and gentle confrontation on the part of the parish.

Educating for Justice

One of the areas of parish life where we tried, with mixed results, to deepen our commitment to justice work is in our experience of Small Christian Communities. Bernard Lee and Michael Cowan, both deeply immersed in both small community work and justice ministries, have consulted our Small Christian Communities and their leaders on the importance of moving their groups toward mercy and justice. Both have cautioned us in small community work about the danger of a kind of spiritual implosion if small communities stay focused just on self-nurture.

Michael Cowan especially has given our groups a methodology for moving toward mercy and justice activity. The steps he suggests are as follows:

1. Take time at a small community meeting to talk about the mercy and justice issues that just will not go away in members' consciousness.

2. Name the concerns that are common to community members.

3. Decide on one area of mercy or justice that all can agree upon for study and activity.

4. Discuss how much time, in addition to the regular faith-sharing the group engages in, this new mercy and justice involvement requires.

5. Decide on the first steps that the Small Christian Community can take in this area.

6. Identify the people of wisdom and experience in this area who might help you get started.

Some of our Small Christian Communities have taken Cowan's strategy and have become involved in varying degrees in mercy and justice projects.

In a similar way, a significant component of our high-school youth ministry involves mercy and justice projects. In the governance structure of youth ministry, two adults are involved as consultants, leading individual teens or our Small Christian Communities for teens (F.L.A.M.E.) into awareness and involvement in mercy and justice projects. When we sit down with young people for interviews before the celebration of their Confirmation, the mercy and justice projects get very positive evaluations.

Frequently over the last two decades I have turned to Thomas Groome's description of religious education to help me understand how evangelization and catechesis can be wed to mercy and justice. In his classic *Christian Religious Education* Groome describes religious education as *political activity, with disciples in time, helping with the emergence of the Reign of God in our midst.*

Groome's description of religious education and ministry reminds us that faith is more than the emotional surrender of Martin Luther's *fiduciary faith,* and more than the creedal clarity of his notion of *intellectual or theoretical faith.* Faith leads to behavior, *behavior that is transformative of society.* The Reign of God emerges in the world. Faith is not a retreat from the world.

Groome has also blessed pastoral ministry with his "shared praxis" methodology of religious education. In this process, a community of disciples of any age, focusing on a particular aspect of our faith, together proceed to appropriate our faith tradition. The first step in this process is discerning community members' starting points relative to the faith issue. The group then moves on to sharing personal stories that might reveal why people are at their given starting point. The process continues toward the proclamation of the Christian story, as the catechist or instructor shares scripture with the group as well as aspects of our faith tradition that are relevant to the topic. The instructor next checks with the group about what is striking them relative to the group sharing. This step is an attempt to articulate the movement of the Holy Spirit as members share faith with each other. The process culminates in a response mode: what should we do, how should we be, based on our faith sharing with each other?

I think the most important part of Groome's last step in shared praxis is the "we" dimension. I sometimes have seen shared praxis used less effectively than it might otherwise have been because it generates only individual responses: What will *I* do? Groome's shared praxis in this response mode can be a natural threshold for a community to become involved in mercy and justice.

We regularly distribute in our parish a statement on political responsibility by the U.S. Catholic bishops entitled *Faithful Citizenship: Civic Responsibility for a New Millennium.* Sometimes using homily time, sometimes in Adult Formation sessions, we remind parishioners of the basic themes of the booklet. The bishops' statement

reminds us that *discipleship involves faithful citizenship*. We are likewise reminded of the richness of the Catholic tradition in mercy and
justice concerns, and that we bring, through everyday experience as
Catholics, a consistent moral framework to the world around us.

This very helpful booklet summarizes the themes of Catholic social teaching: the life and dignity of the human person; the call to
family, community, and participation; human rights, but also human
responsibilities for the well-being of society; disciples' option for the
poor and vulnerable; the dignity of work and the rights of workers;
Jesus' call to us to move toward solidarity with one another; and care
for God's creation.

The document also discusses moral priorities for our shared public life: protecting human life; protecting family life; pursuing social
justice; practicing global solidarity. We regularly ask parishioners
around election time to use this document in their selection of candidates for public office whose policies seem closest to Jesus' vision of
the Reign of God.

In January 2006 we began yet another attempt at immersing ourselves in justice and social ministry. Some years ago Jack Jazreal and
Catholic Charities U.S.A. began to produce materials entitled "Just-
Faith." JustFaith is a thirty-week program in which participants in
Small Christian Communities learn about issues of justice and social ministry, while simultaneously being involved in works of mercy
and justice. Several of us in leadership studied this model for use
with adults. A comparable program, JWalking, or JusticeWalking, is
offered for teens.

JustFaith now has a network of over three hundred parishes
participating. The program combines education on the church's social teachings and social ministry, small community experience, and
actual involvement in service.

Holy Family determined that a thirty-week program was too stren-
uous for our parishioners, involved in so many ministries and small
communities already. Rather, as part of our winter program, Foundations: The Search for Jesus, we offered a series on four Mondays
called "Faith That Does Justice." It was an interactive formation series, which I facilitated with leaders from the Service, Justice and

Peace Leadership Community. The topics we covered included: An Overview of Catholic Social Teaching; The Crisis of Hunger, Homelessness, and Poverty; Labor and Economic Justice; The Crime of Punishment; and Practical Steps for Justice Involvement.

This was followed during the spring by another series, five weeks in length, co-sponsored by Holy Family and Catholic Relief Services entitled "Salt and Light." In this series we went into great depth in Catholic social teaching.

This formational period on mercy and justice concluded in June of 2006 with a retreat day entitled "The Foundations of Justice." The day focused on local and global opportunities for justice involvement.

Jim Wallis, in his classic *The Call to Conversion*, reminds us that two things are necessary for a faith community to grow in justice and mercy. The first is actually being with those who are suffering from injustice, and the second is making the needs and issues of mercy and justice a regular part of the prayer life of a community.

As I mentioned earlier, architecturally we have tried to express a commitment to mercy and justice. On either side of our worship space are two small gathering areas. On the right side as you enter there is a chapel for twenty-four-hour, seven-day-a-week Eucharistic devotion. On the other side is the Mercy and Justice Room, containing literature and audiovisual resources on issues of mercy and justice, on our seven areas of concern, and on the ministries that Holy Family has taken on in these areas. In our architecture we are trying to capture Richard Rohr's challenge to us to be people of contemplation and action for justice.

Chapter Nine

A Church for Youth
and Young Adults

ONE OF THE GREATEST challenges facing parishes in the twenty-first century is the evangelization of adolescents and young adults. Here also the Catholic Church finds itself woefully behind the times and underdeveloped in its strategies.

A memo recently came across my desk from the archdiocese, announcing that "the Catholic Youth Office has been closed. . . . " This is one of the radical budget cuts in archdiocesan ministry resources due to dwindling funds.

As Catholic leaders obsess about the ritualistic details of implementing the General Instruction for the Roman Missal and changing the language of the sacramentary to more "Latin-sounding English," teens and young adults honestly lament the boring nature of most Catholic worship. Aging clergy, growing farther and farther away from adolescents, and often with inept preaching skills, are unable to connect with young people. The low salaries and inadequate pastoral management provided youth ministers make the position of youth minister a revolving door in most parishes, with youth ministers usually staying in a faith community only two or three years. Youth ministers have very little power on pastoral staffs and lack authority.

Though I am now one of the aging clergy and perhaps do not connect with youth as effectively as I used to, youth ministry has always been a top priority for me as a parish priest. In recent years, while I try to be pastorally present to youth at their various events, I see it as more my responsibility to insure that quality youth ministry takes place in the parish by sharing my vision, hiring professional ministers to implement the vision, and calling forth parishioners to care for young people.

One of the resources that challenged me the most regarding youth ministry when I was younger was Erik Erikson's "epigenetic" theory of human development. Recall Erikson's stages:

1. The stage of infancy is characterized by the tension between trust and mistrust.

2. Post-infancy is characterized by the conflict between autonomy and shame or doubt.

3. The pre-school years are characterized by the tension between initiation and guilt.

4. The early school years, or the fourth stage, are characterized by the tension between industry and inferiority.

5. Adolescence is the fifth stage, containing within it the conflict between identity and identity confusion. Erikson felt that the stage of adolescence recapitulates all that has gone on before in human development, while pushing the individual onward to the adult stages of life.

6. The sixth stage is characterized by intimacy vs. isolation. This is the stage of young adulthood.

7. The seventh stage, or midlife, is characterized by the conflict between generativity and stagnation.

8. In the eighth stage, or the senior years, older adults wrestle with integrity vs. despair.

Within Erikson's stage of adolescence, there are seven additional subconflicts or tensions:

• Temporal perspective vs. time confusion. Adolescents develop a handle on their future, or they are paralyzed by the future.

• Self-certainty vs. self-consciousness. Adolescents strive to have a healthy self-confidence, or they hang back in a restrictive sense of self-deprecation.

- Role experimentation vs. role fixation. The adolescent years are a time to experiment with many different personas rather than being fixed in a single self-concept.

- Apprenticeship vs. work paralysis. Adolescence ought to be a time when young people are encouraged to explore their giftedness and the needs of the world around them. Adolescence is a time to focus on vocation, or one's calling.

- Bisexual polarization vs. bisexual confusion. Adolescence is a time to develop positive feelings about oneself as a male or a female.

- Leadership/followership vs. authority confusion. Adolescence is a time for being mentored. In a generative way, adults ought to serve as markers for adolescents as they try to find their way to adulthood. Unfortunately, generative adults are often not emotionally available for adolescents. This includes parents and other authority figures.

- Ideological commitment vs. confusion of values. The teen years are an important time to articulate ideals, conscience, and moral principles that one will live by. It also is a time when values and morals can become fudged or underdeveloped, usually because of a lack of input.

Robert Coles, in his pioneering work on the morality of young people, talks about the importance of *moral conversations* in moral development. He says that all of us grow in conscience by having moral conversations, especially with trusted mentors. The absence of moral conversations results in stunted moral development. Many Americans are becoming God-deprived and live more by the values of the dominant culture than by what Jesus meant by the Reign of God.

Erikson, Coles, and others remind us of the uniquely spiritual nature of the stage of adolescence. Adolescents are not necessarily religious in an organized, institutional way, but they are beginning to develop the mental ability to deal with profound spiritual and moral principles.

At this deeply spiritual period, parish churches frequently offer little or nothing to help adolescents grow as disciples of Jesus Christ.

Because of this many Catholic youth have moved toward evangelical churches. Though their fundamentalist theology and spirituality might be dreadful, these organizations nonetheless offer Catholic youth "another place" to hang out, genuine experiences of community, heartfelt worship, and systematic formation as disciples of Jesus.

Often these evangelical churches use a methodology very close to the steps of the Rite of Christian Initiation of Adults. They probably do not understand or know the history of the RCIA, but they have come upon the same kinds of steps because the catechumenal process is such a natural, spiritual socialization process.

In the 1980s and 1990s, when I was serving as director for the Office for Chicago Catholic Evangelization, Dawn Mayer, the associate director at the time, and I began to offer to parishes and clusters of parishes a methodology for wholistic youth ministry. Rather than a pre-set program, this was more a discipline for doing youth ministry. We called it F.L.A.M.E., an acronym for Friendship, Leadership, Acceptance, Ministry, and Education. Since that time, I have brought the process to Holy Family Parish. Over 350 high-school teens are part of the process, with another close to 300 junior high students in a parallel process.

F.L.A.M.E. seeks to minister to young people through the discipline of the RCIA. Thus, there are regular experiences for pre-evangelization and evangelization. Intergenerational Small Christian Communities provide opportunities for meaningful catechesis on the appropriate developmental level. There is a period of proximate preparation for those who wish, as well as a period of purification and enlightenment for those who choose to be confirmed or to complete the journey of their own initiation into the church. There is an annual celebration of the Sacrament of Confirmation. We also have begun better follow-up after Confirmation, providing opportunities for Small Christian Communities and catechesis for older teens.

Sprinkled throughout the process are retreats that are developmentally shaped for teens. We recently have added the famous Kairos model for older teens.

Let's look at the F.L.A.M.E. model in a little more detail. The evangelization of young people is accomplished through two ministries. As with all our ministries, youth ministries have a leader, a co-leader, and a Ministering Community. As best we can, we try to make all the ministries involved in F.L.A.M.E. intergenerational, with *peer ministers* assuming leadership in the various ministries, while being mentored in leadership by adults.

Under the umbrella of evangelization, T.O.R.C.H., an acronym for Teens Out to Reach Christian Hearts, sponsors social events for parish teens and their friends. These social events involve going someplace together or doing something together as a large group. One of the more popular events is a touch football game held every Friday after Thanksgiving, which attracts hundreds of teens.

"Ignite" is a large group event. A dynamic speaker is brought in to speak about Jesus or some aspect of the mysteries of Christianity. The speaker is usually accompanied by Christian music. Christian music has become so important at Holy Family that we regularly host Christian music concerts for the parish and for the entire metropolitan area. From non-Catholics in attendance we often get reactions like, "We didn't think Catholic churches did things like this."

F.L.A.M.E. Small Christian Communities are made up of twelve to fifteen teens, one or two peer ministers, and an adult mentor or catechist. The materials that are used for faith sharing and learning in F.L.A.M.E. groups have varied over the years. At this writing, there are currently minicourse materials on Jesus, scripture, church, prayer and spirituality, morality, and human sexuality. Regular mentor/catechist formation, as well as peer minister training and formation, is vital for making these small communities work.

Celebrating the Spirit is a parallel process that some teens choose to enter for proximate preparation for completing their initiation into the church through Confirmation. These various programs are not a high-school Confirmation program. They are a full-cycle youth ministry that includes the possibility of confirming one's faith if one so wishes.

Teens involved in Celebrating the Spirit attend a Teen/Sponsor dinner and also meet with me to talk about the meaning of Confirmation and reasons for choosing to be confirmed. A two-day Confirmation retreat follows. Opportunities to participate in projects of mercy and justice are presented. We call these projects Y.E.S. projects (Youth Experiencing Service).

After Confirmation, thirty-five to fifty teens, on average, go on to become peer ministers the following year. Many teens choose a ministry from among the eight divisions of ministry explained earlier. In addition, there are Small Christian Communities for juniors and seniors who have been confirmed called Living the Fire groups.

The evangelization of youth, indeed all evangelization, ought to be mission driven. A parish ought to call its youth to a decision for Jesus Christ and a commitment to begin responsible membership in the Body of Christ, the church. A process moving toward the celebration of the Sacrament of Confirmation can help facilitate such a commitment. Most of us know that Confirmation is a sacrament seeking a theology and practice. Let's consider for a moment all that the Sacrament of Confirmation can be.

Confirmation can be a celebration of new awareness of the Holy Spirit in one's life and in the life of the community, a celebration of personal and communal Pentecost.

Confirmation can be the celebration of the completion of one's initiation into the Body of Christ. In the case of most adolescents, the first two steps of initiation, namely, Baptism and Eucharist, were determined by the parents.

Confirmation can be the beginning of adult faith. Our young people are not adults, but they are beginning to know what some of the rights and responsibilities of adulthood are, and that can be celebrated in this sacrament.

We also celebrate in Confirmation the giftedness of the people being confirmed, their sharing in the power and the gifts of the Holy Spirit. A Confirmation process ought to allow sufficient time for discernment of one's gifts.

Like all of the sacraments, Confirmation should lead to mission. Whether it is in one's faith community, at school, or in the world beyond, young people who have been confirmed should want to be about the work of the Reign of God. A Confirmation process should help young people understand what Jesus meant by the Reign of God.

The steps of our full-cycle youth evangelization efforts are these: the pre-evangelization and evangelization steps of T.O.R.C.H. and Ignite; the communal/catechetical step of F.L.A.M.E.; the proximate preparation/purification period of Celebrating the Spirit; and the programs of Small Christian Communities for juniors and seniors (Living the Fire), peer ministry, and training for discerned ministries.

Some twenty years ago I found it interesting how these Roman Catholic, RCIA-style steps of youth ministry parallel similar steps of youth ministry in evangelical churches. The classical steps of evangelical youth ministry are (1) appeal to young people on the level of fun-seekers; (2) help them to become spiritually sensitive; (3) invite them to seek out what it means to be a Christian; (4) invite them further to become disciples of Jesus Christ. In the third and fourth steps, there usually is a baptism-like ceremony, even if the young people have been baptized already as infants. The ceremony, usually done by immersion in a pool of water, celebrates their decision and their commitment to be for Christ. There then is a follow-up that manifests itself in many different ways, the step of *becoming workers* for Christ.

If parishes do not want to use Confirmation as a step in youth ministry, I encourage them to devise some other ritual for making a public commitment to Jesus, the Reign of God, and the Body of Christ, the church.

We have a responsibility to reach out to as many young people as possible. With about seven hundred young people that we minister to, we probably are reaching only one-third of our *Roman Catholic* potential, not even considering unchurched teens and families.

The F.L.A.M.E. groups are catechetical groups, groups in which awakened faith seeks understanding or deepening. These groups are lectionary-based. Part of the two-hour session is devoted to breaking open next Sunday's Word. Here also we see the prevailing Eucharist-hubbed attitude of all of our parish ministries. In behavior, the Eucharist is spoken of and experienced as our source and summit of faith.

The catechetical content of F.L.A.M.E. groups is put together by our Youth Ministry staff. The material takes the form of mini-courses that the teens experience together.

We are working, in adolescent catechesis, on building into the process some experiences of *Catholic apologetics.* Through testing in some aspects of the Creed, the memorization of certain core truths, and deeper understanding of faith, teens are being empowered to be able to *talk* about their faith.

On a weekend that was marked by the archdiocese as "Evangelization Sunday" I encouraged each of our parishioners to write a personal mission statement about their involvement with Jesus, the Reign of God, and the Body of Christ. An outline was provided on how to go about writing such a mission statement. I explained at each Mass that the goal of articulating a faith mission statement was to use it, at some appropriate time, to share faith with others, especially with people who seem to be in a time of their lives in which they need the support and help that an active faith life can bring.

I wanted to encourage teens as well as people of all ages to be better positioned to engage in apologetics (that is, talking about one's faith); and then to evangelize, or to invite someone to a deeper relationship with Christ, attendance at our church, or more regular involvement in our church.

40 Assets

I remind the reader that in all of our ministries with children, teens, and families, Holy Family has made a commitment to share, especially with parents, but also with children and teens, the 40 Developmental Assets developed by the Search Institute in Minneapolis. Research has proven that the more of these assets that young people develop and are helped to develop, the less inclined they will be to engage in irresponsible sexual activity, drug or alcohol use, and a violent approach to their problems and crises.

As I said in another chapter, asset development needs to begin early on in childhood. In recent years, many materials have been developed for the development of the assets in early and middle childhood.

As part of our involvement in the Assets, a few years ago we surveyed a number of our teens regarding where they were relative to the assets. While many of our young people displayed a number of the Developmental Assets, some of the deficits that were reported were as follows:

- A significant number of our young people at the time were binge drinking.

- A number reported giving little or no time to reading or the arts.

- A number reported feeling an emotional distance from their parents.

- A number reported not feeling valued by the adults in their schools, neighborhoods, and church.

Some of the adults to whom I presented this material did not want to accept that this information described their young people. But at least twice in my time at Holy Family, large drug and alcohol parties had to be broken up by the police.

Part of the difficulty in building a healthy Catholic youth ministry is the lack of leadership and resources on diocesan levels. The development of healthy youth ministries has become largely each parish's responsibility. When I worked for the archdiocese I experimented with creating supportive networks of parishes. The idea behind these alliances is to get parishes to support each other in learning excellent strategies for parish life. Youth ministry is one of those areas that could certainly benefit from collaboration and swapping models, efforts, and ideas.

Another problem in building youth ministry, as already mentioned, is the revolving door nature of youth ministers. Often, youth ministers are right out of college, poorly paid, and not properly trained for youth ministry. Thus, many youth ministers focus on a relatively small group of teens that becomes the "youth group," while literally hundreds go un-touched, un-evangelized, un-catechized by the parish.

Recently our current co-directors of youth ministries preached at all the Masses, calling for teens and adults in the parish to step forward to help with the youth work at Holy Family. In the front of the church and on the pillars hung the names of the over seven hundred teens from junior and senior high school who currently participate in our programs. As the two co-directors called for people to step forward to minister to these seven hundred young people, I reminded the congregation that the seven hundred probably represented only a third of just the Catholic potential out there.

In hiring professional people for youth ministry, I no longer speak of the director of youth *ministry*. I speak of the director or co-directors of youth *ministries*. As I hope this chapter has explained, to adequately minister to youth, multiple ministries must be offered in the areas of evangelization, catechesis, worship, pastoral care, mercy and justice, and other ministries represented in the parish.

The role of a director or co-director is to not do everything "for" the young people. While doing some direct ministry to young people, the director and co-directors must call forth, empower, and train many of the baptized to do youth ministry work.

I encourage all of us to hear the call of Jesus in Mark 10: "Let the children, the young people come to me. Do nothing to stop them."

Young Adult Ministry

We in Catholic leadership are constantly hearing and reading about the success of evangelical megachurches, especially in evangelizing young adults. What is the attraction of these churches to people in their twenties and thirties?

Though theologically we might criticize evangelicals, the evangelical churches do a good job at a kind of foundational evangelization. They introduce people to a personal and communal relationship with Jesus that is close and available. They solidify that relationship with Christ with multi-layered relationships with members of the church, emphasizing membership in Small Christian Communities or small groups. It is in these small groups that evangelicals "close the evangelical back door," not allowing new members to enter the front door and exit quickly. Young adults are also quickly invited into membership in ministry and service organizations in the congregation. Perhaps most importantly, young adults are invited to worship services that provide a heartfelt religious experience consisting of dramatic and effective teaching and preaching, as well as upbeat Christian music that stirs young spirits.

Young adults are welcomed into multi-generational evangelical congregations. The churches are not focused only on young adults. These churches understand that young adults are not all of one kind. There are college age young adults, single young adults, married young adults, young adults with questions unique to those in their twenties, young adults with questions unique to those in their thirties, young adults making the transition from late adolescence to early young adulthood, young adults making the transition into their thirties, young adults making the transition from young adulthood to midlife. Whether we are talking about Catholic young adult ministry or evangelical young adult ministry, all of these age and demographic factors must be taken into consideration to adequately evangelize young adults.

I asked someone in archdiocesan leadership recently how many full-time young adult ministers were on staffs in the Archdiocese of Chicago. I was told that our parish, Holy Family Parish, was the only parish that had a full-time young adult minister. In other congregations, other professionals are doing the work of young adult ministry, but do not have the time or job description to focus only on young adults.

At Holy Family, we try to employ some of the dynamics that have proven successful for evangelical congregations, while also developing our own unique young adult Catholic culture. To do young adult ministry well, the young adult minister must multiply his or her services many times over through the kind of empowerment that I described earlier in this book.

At Holy Family we offer a variety of programs to evangelize our young adults. There are social ministries for the important pre-evangelization work of building up relationships. There are opportunities for young adults to be in Small Christian Communities with other young adults, or with other age groups.

There is a ministry that focuses on the first five years of marriage, which the Creighton study, *Time, Sex, and Money,* of 2000 has said contains the highest divorce rate of any age group in America today. According to the Creighton study, time starvation, dissatisfaction with the sexual relationship, and debts brought into the marriage from previous years contribute to discord in the marriage. Suggestions are also offered on how to address these challenges and keep intimacy growing.

We have also tried non-Eucharistic worship services presided over by young adults, allowing them to offer their reflections and break open the Word. Young adults also serve as wonderful consultants and mentors to young people in high-school youth ministry. In some instances, they become part of the intergenerational team that leads F.L.A.M.E. groups for high-school students.

Retreats are important for young adults. At Holy Family, we offer retreats on a variety of levels. We have a ministry to our college age young adults, especially those attending commuter colleges in the area. Retreats, Masses on the campus of a local commuter college where permissible, and visitation of other campuses are among the efforts invested in by the parish. While young adults have had a regular involvement in our 5:00 p.m. Sunday afternoon Mass for some years, following a model from Old St. Pat's in downtown Chicago we began this fall a once-a-month 11:00 a.m. Mass, open to the entire parish, that is planned and ministered by the young adult community.

In many Catholic and Protestant congregations and parishes, the culture, the environment, is not a contagious, evangelizing, welcoming, exciting, nurturing one that young adults cry out for. Many young adults are bored with their churches. It is not that they are angry or hurt or alienated. They are bored and apathetic. Catholic young adult ministry is episodic, anemic, inadequate, lacking in any serious planning, goals, or objectives.

The bishops' young adult document of 1997, *Sons and Daughters of the Light,* offers some lofty ideals about young adult ministry: that young adult ministry should lead young adults to a personal relationship with Jesus, to responsible membership in their parish church, and to see their work in the world as part of a mission of the

Reign of God. I embrace these ideals and think that they are good ones, but most Catholic parishes, and many Protestant congregations, have much work to do in terms of pastoral planning, the hiring of professional ministers, and the empowerment of young adult laity, if these ideals are ever to become reality.

In our pastoral plan, *New Image of Parish (Revised)*, our parish has made a commitment to grow young adult ministry involvement by 25 percent every year for the next five years.

Chapter Ten

The Convergence Model
in Action

E ARLIER IN THE BOOK I talked about how Holy Family has over
150 ministries. Each of those ministries finds its home in one of
eight divisions of ministry. Again, the eight divisions are Adult Formation, Evangelical Outreach, Family F.A.I.T.H. and Life, Pastoral
Care, Youth Ministries, Worship, Operations, and Service, Justice and
Peace. These eight divisions converge for one mission: evangelization.

I want to highlight in this chapter how the different personnel in
each division relate with each other.

Each division of ministry, or Leadership Community for ministry,
is led by a director or co-directors. In some of the Leadership Communities there are also associate directors. Historically we have also
had coordinators in some of the divisions, with lesser responsibilities
than the associate directors. The ministry staff is assisted in its work
by the administrative staff. The staff and the people of the parish
are also served by the maintenance staff, who attend to the practical
needs of the parish plant.

Directors meet weekly. The ministry staff meets once a month.
The ministry staff also meets once a month for a Word and Worship
gathering. These meetings are an attempt to keep everything that we
do congruent with and connected to the liturgy and the liturgical
year. "All Staff" is a gathering of the ministry, administrative, and
maintenance staffs, either for debriefing, faith formation and training,
or open discussions of issues in the parish.

All in parish leadership meet on the second Tuesday of the month
for business and/or training and faith formation. Two years ago,
our training and faith formation was in the area of parish-based

evangelization. We asked the question, *How can our parish become a more truly evangelizing community?* The result of our research, as well as of focus group meetings and town hall meetings with parishioners, was our new five-year plan, *New Image of Parish (Revised)*.

Last year our Leadership Communities studied Rick Warren's book *The Purpose Driven Church,* constantly asking ourselves the questions, Where are we purpose driven? Where do we need to grow in purpose and mission?

This upcoming year our sessions will focus on a spirituality and strategies for stewardship. This program will run parallel to intensive efforts at fundraising for two needs before us: the renovation of our church space, and the construction of a new Center for Children, Youth, and Families, which will house our Family F.A.I.T.H. Ministries, Holy Family Catholic Academy, and Holy Family Youth Ministries.

Structures need to fit the mission of an organization, and structures need to be flexible and changeable, based on changing needs and culture. Our Leadership Communities' structures have changed several times in the ten years that I have been pastor.

The most recent change came out of our year of evangelization study. Though all eight Leadership Communities converge on the wholistic mission of evangelization, we felt we needed to take the ministries that seem to interact more with the unchurched, under-churched, bored, apathetic, marginalized people that somehow are connected with Holy Family, and unite them under one umbrella or Leadership Community. Largely these ministries had originated in a previous adult faith formation structure.

Adult Faith Formation was streamlined into three categories:

- the ministries connected with our School of Ministry;

- retreat/spiritual renewal ministries; and

- marriage enrichment.

The new Evangelical Outreach Community has been divided into two categories. The first we call Relational Ministries, which include Support for Annulment; Baptismal Preparation of parents bringing their children for Baptism; Bible Study groups; the Center for Inner Peace, Hope, Forgiveness, and Reconciliation; the Catholic Family Movement; Community on Wednesday, which is a non-Eucharistic faith formation event for adults and families; Foundations, a series we began eight years ago for those feeling under-catechized; Landings, which reaches out to inactive, possibly returning Catholics; Mini-Retreats, which we are developing to help families understand what it means to be responsible members of a parish church; Multi-Cultural Ministry; Neighborhood Ministry; Parish Missions; Pathways, a group for single people; Footsteps in Faith, our approach to the RCIA; Rising from Divorce, an educational series for those in the process of emotional divorce; Small Christian Communities; Young Adult Ministry; Welcoming of Newcomers; and the Welcoming/Concierge Ministry, which is the servicing of a Welcoming Desk in the narthex of our church (called the Family Room) to help newcomers or visitors find their way around our campus.

The second division of Evangelical Outreach is Communications Ministries. One of our staff members has the sole responsibility of producing and managing audio/visual materials. This person serves as the producer of our Radio, TV, and Internet Ministries. For the last twenty-five years, Dawn Mayer, our pastoral associate, and I have hosted a radio show called *Horizons,* a lectionary-based program looking at each Sunday's readings, with contemporary popular music interspersed in our commentary. We now videotape the radio show and play that on cable access TV in close to sixty suburbs in the Chicago area.

We have begun our own Internet radio station called *The Stream,* through which people with personal computers can connect with a variety of programs and talks that have been given at the parish. We also have begun developing a team of youth for the production of audiovisual materials for adolescents.

We have opened our own bookstore to help people stay connected with quality reading material, Christian music, and devotional objects. We have just made our very inspiring and controversial cross, The Cross of New Life, depicting Jesus beginning to rise from death as he dies on the cross. It is available in quite affordable models for devotion at home.

We have begun to connect quantitative objectives to some of our goals. Some of the areas we are targeting for increased numbers are Young Adult Ministry, Small Christian Communities, and Neighborhood Ministry. Also in the area of Neighborhood Ministry, we have just hired another priest to work with me in this effort, especially to make neighborhood liturgies more available to our parishioners.

Each Leadership Community has a leader and a co-leader, the co-leader most frequently apprenticing to be the leader in two or three years. Each Leadership Community is made up of a number of smaller units called Ministering Communities, each with a leader and apprenticing co-leader, and a number of parishioners who serve in that given Ministering Community. Each of the Leadership Communities selects and sends a representative from each Leadership Community to the Pastoral Council.

This relationship between Ministering Communities, Leadership Communities, Pastoral Council, and pastoral staff has provided for us a remarkable harnessing of gifts and energy for servant leadership in the parish. This harnessing is what I call the convergence model of evangelization.

If there is any challenge in this model, it is to keep repeating the vision and practice over and over again, since new people are constantly becoming active in ministry. To the degree that we have presumed over the years that everyone knows and understands the model, we have become not as effective and efficient as we could have been. Thus, with the beginning of each academic year, I take time at Leadership Community meetings to retell the story of the birth and development of our structure and style of being and doing parish.

Again, the structure is at the service of our vision, mission, and heart values or principles.

Chapter Eleven

Re-Imagining the Priesthood and New Pastoral Roles

THE PRIESTHOOD as we know it today has evolved over the last two thousand years. Ministry in the early church was begun by the apostles, who became missionaries to different parts of the world. As Christian communities multiplied, ministry was characterized more by charisms than office. Acts 2 gives us a glimpse of the church at its birth, with all disciples seeing themselves as servants.

As Christian communities grew, the need for greater organization emerged. The role of deacon, dedicated to pastoral ministry, and bishop, or overseer, developed in many communities. Bishops seem to have been more common in communities influenced by Greek culture. In communities converting from Judaism to Christianity, a role that became important was that of elder, or presbyter, or priest.

In the first centuries of Christianity, it was not necessarily bishops or priests who presided at the Eucharist. The identity of presiders at the Eucharist is unclear, but those who presided were chosen by the local community. Some historians suggest that the head of the household would preside at a Eucharist held in that person's home. According to some theories this could have been a male or a female. By the end of the second century, it seems that only the bishop, or one delegated by the bishop, could preside at the Eucharist.

By the end of the third century, the roles of presbyter, bishop, and deacon were solidified. Also by the end of the third century, we witness the emergence of the monarchical episcopate, with a bishop presiding over a local church, or what came to be known as a diocese. The role of the presbyterate was to share in the ministry of the bishop, allowing his ministry to be expanded to many more people.

129

Eventually the deaconate ceased to exist, except as a transitional step to the priesthood.

There is historical evidence that the role of deaconess existed in the early Christian centuries. As I mentioned earlier, some Orthodox-rite churches are in the process of reviving the ministry of deaconess.

The priesthood became a composite role of bishop/pastor, minister of the word, sacramental minister, and presider at the Eucharist. The priesthood went through a period in which it was very much shaped by feudalism. Not only did priests have their obviously religious tasks to do, but they also collected taxes for their feudal lords and took direction from their feudal lords more than they did the bishops.

It was not until the year 1208 that there is evidence of a requirement of priestly ordination to preside at the Eucharist. This was issued by Pope Innocent III. This was made more official at the Council of Florence in 1439 and the Council of Trent in 1563.

Priestly celibacy was not a legal requirement for the priesthood until the twelfth century. While there probably were a number of motivating factors in moving toward mandatory celibacy, there was a very practical one: that church property not fall into the hands of priests' wives and children upon their deaths. Let it be clear that celibacy has always been a gift, held in high esteem and regard in the church, but it is not a gift that has been joined by divine will to the ordained priesthood.

Shortage of Priests

As of this writing, the average age of priests in the United States is in the late fifties. A significant number of men have left the priesthood in the last thirty-five to forty years. The numbers of those being ordained are far fewer than when I was ordained in 1973.

There are a myriad of reasons for the clergy shortage. Because of the mood and atmosphere in church life today, few priests encourage young men to consider the priesthood. Significant also, as parents look on the turbulent waters that the priesthood is in, few parents encourage their children to consider life in ministry. The sexual scandals damaged the image of the priesthood, probably irreparably.

Andrew Greeley in *Priest: A Calling in Crisis* and Donald Cozzens in *Faith That Dares to Speak* both highlight "clerical culture" as a significant problem for the present and the future of the priesthood. Priests still live in a separated, caste-like system, presumably ontologically different from the laity. This has led to considerable intrapsychic, interpersonal dysfunction, and, Greeley would add, a severe lack of professionalism in executing the priestly duties of preaching, teaching, presiding, and sharing the sacraments.

William Bausch, in his popular book *Brave New Church*, wrote in the year 2001 that "the bishops would rather issue pastoral letters, deny the Eucharist to their people, blend beloved parishes, and overwork their priests with each succeeding year, than face Rome, or publicly raise the taboo subject of a married clergy." He speaks of submissiveness, betrayal, and pastoral cowardice.

Richard Gaillardetz, in his book *By What Authority?* (2003), encourages the church to embrace what which Vatican II spoke of so beautifully and poetically, the *sensus fidelium,* or the sense of the faithful. The council leaders emphasized that the gifts and wisdom of the Spirit certainly are present among bishops and priests, but also among all those who are baptized. Gaillardetz calls for a movement from a juridical model of pastoral life to a communal model that would involve much more discernment and discussion, on all levels of church, regarding issues vital to the Christian life.

I do not think the "magic pill" for what troubles the church is that all clergy should get married, or be allowed to marry. If a person who wants to be a priest also feels called to the married life, I hope and pray that that person will be able to follow both vocations. But I also believe that some priests, based on personality type, would be horrible husbands. Perhaps larger questions than simply, "Should priests be allowed to marry?" should be entertained in worldwide contemplative conversations. Among the questions are these:

- What are the qualities or gifts in a person that would qualify that person to preside at Eucharist?

- What kind of gifts are needed for a person to be an effective preacher?

- What gifts are needed to pastor a parish?

- What gifts are needed to preside over and administer the other sacraments besides the Eucharist?

- What does the ideal pastoral staff look like?

- How did Jesus treat women?

- How would Jesus treat women today in his church?

- Why is the Catholic Church closing and blending parishes and schools, while evangelical churches are multiplying, expanding, and attracting Catholics?

Much of what priests do can be done by others who genuinely possess the gifts needed for the ministerial tasks.

Many Ministries

If we look at what troubles us through the lens of rigid ideologies, we will not successfully address our problems and crises for decades, and the Catholic Church will continue its downward slide. A better approach to discernment and discussion is to address pastoral needs and the gifts required to address those needs.

Vatican II reminded the church that ordained priests share in the ministry or priesthood of their local ordinary or bishop. In turn, it has been my experience in all the parishes that I have served in, but most of all in this parish that I have pastored, that parishioners share in my priesthood, and all of us, connected with the archbishop of Chicago, are really sharing in and continuing the mission, the work, the priesthood, if you will, of Jesus Christ.

The staff at Holy Family very effectively serves this community. The staff at Holy Family challenges parishes to think out of the box, to think in new categories, to use new language in ministering to a parish.

I work with a director of operations who cares for most of the business end of parish life and also takes care of personnel issues and the management of the campus.

I have a director of finances who is responsible for all the stewardship issues of parish life.

I work with a director of Family F.A.I.T.H. and Life who ministers to over thirteen hundred children and their parents in the ministries of religious education.

I have a director of youth ministries who cares for approximately seven hundred junior high and high-school students.

A number of associate directors work with me in Evangelical Outreach.

There is a director of service, justice, and peace, who is constantly prompting the parish to become more invested in the works of mercy and justice.

Our director of pastoral care animates many people to care for the sick, the dying, and the bereaved, and encourages people to embrace a discipline for wellness.

Our director of adult faith trains people for ministry, invites them to ongoing adult spiritual renewal, and tries to enrich marriage and home life.

Our director of worship animates hundreds of people to truly make the Eucharist the source and summit of our faith.

I am not saying that these categories that we have landed upon are necessarily the right categories for every parish. Sometimes I am dismissed at clergy conferences because priests pessimistically say, "The only way a structure like yours can work is because of the finances that you have at your parish." But I have used similar structures in every parish that I have worked in, and some of those parishes could be described as middle class, lower middle class, or even upper lower income. I ask readers only to listen for the heart values that I am espousing and then to engage in creative thinking and action to translate them into their own faith communities.

Epilogue

The Wittenberg Door

ON APRIL 13, 2005, Andrew Greeley wrote an article from Rome for the *Chicago Sun-Times*. He was on assignment covering the election of the new pope. Greeley brought up a theme that I have touched on in this book and in other writings, a theme popularized by Gerald Arbuckle some years ago, that our church, for some time now, has been in a restorationist mode rather than a re-birthing or re-imagining mode. Greeley captured the dynamics of restorationism by declaring that the bishops at the conclave act and speak as if Vatican II never happened, or if it did, it was insignificant.

Greeley counters that Vatican II and its wonderful documents changed the church forever and demonstrated the weakness of the hierarchical and clerical culture and its attempts to move the church back to a pre–Vatican II style. The church that many people grew up in during the 1960s, 1970s, and 1980s was an open, inclusive church, a church with a self-concept that all are the people of God, all Christians are the church, all Christians are the Body of Christ, and that the *sensus fidelium* was an important dynamic in church teaching.

Richard McBrien, in articles written in June and July 2005, critiques the leaders of the church for taking their extreme, right-wing approach and claiming it is the centrist position in the church. Those of us who have considered ourselves centrists are being pushed to the left and stereotyped as extreme. With this political maneuvering, many of us who strive to create healthy structures in the parish, who try to uncover what Jesus meant when he taught about the Reign of God, are marginalized, judged harshly, and are not invited in for dialogue or collaboration on important archdiocesan or church matters.

When I was doing doctoral work in theology and pastoral ministry in the late 1970s, I was struck by one instructor who repetitively referred to the challenge of "being committed to the Reign of God without falling into ideology." He was calling us, as a learning community, to a kind of *searching faith* that strives to interpret life and the world around us through Jesus' teachings about God's Reign.

It is very easy for religious people to fall into ideology. Ideology is the opposite of searching faith. Ideology is taking some timebound, human-made derivative ideas from a faith tradition and treating them as if they are divine truths. Ideology is a kind of misguided "group think" rather than common sense. Ideology leads to harsh judgment of others who do not share the same ideas. Ideology leads to biases and prejudices.

Religious people who get involved in ideology rather than searching for divine truth create religious systems that *screen people out,* people who do not hold to the ideas of the ideologues. John Savage, in his book on non-practicing Christians, *The Apathetic and Bored Church Member,* highlights the phenomenon of "screening congregations."

After extensive research, Savage wrote that many non-practicing, "fallen away" people feel that they do not fit the job description of what it means to be a practicing Christian, or practicing Catholic. They feel screened out by the prevailing ideology. Some are divorced. Some have practiced birth control. Some are homosexual. Some are in a second marriage. Some are women who feel God is calling them to a more responsible role in church leadership. Some have questions about the status of leadership in our church. Some are young adults who feel that the aging church they grew up in neither understands nor cares about their age group. Some are adolescents who naturally have a searching faith, which is not encouraged by the church or parish.

Savage says those who feel screened out by ideology are not necessarily hurt or angry with the church. They become *bored and apathetic toward it,* and they reinvest their spiritually searching energy in other areas.

As Jesus preached the Reign of God, he preached a vision of life that was inclusive, open to all types of people. This particularly troubled the Pharisees, who had become paralyzed by ideology. The Pharisees felt that they alone were adequately keeping the law, which they confused with God's law and God's truth. They held in judgment anyone who did not think as they did. Neighboring peoples, like Canaanites, Samaritans, those they classified as "the Gentiles," were not to be interacted with.

Along comes Jesus, who not only interacts with the non-Pharisees, but reaches out to them and teaches them that God's Reign is theirs. When Jesus refers to the Canaanite woman in the Gospel of Matthew with the word "dog," I believe he is being tongue in cheek. He is saying that the Pharisees look on the Canaanite woman as a dog, but he sees in her a profound faith, a faith that connects with his healing power to heal her daughter.

The message of inclusiveness and universalism regarding the Reign of God is also found in Isaiah, where, through the prophetic writer, God says that foreigners are going to be accepted into God's Reign. Similarly, Paul speaks of himself in Romans as the "apostle for the Gentiles," one who has been sent to preach the good news of the Reign of God to a non-Pharisaical, non-Jewish world.

Dysfunctional Leadership

In what ways may the Catholic Church be a screening phenomenon? More particularly, in what ways might our parishes be screening congregations? Who, perhaps, does not fit because of the "job description" we have collectively created for parish membership?

Let's pray for God's help that, as a church and parishes, we will not be crippled by ideology, but rather embrace a commitment to searching faith. It is so easy for us to look on Islam and speak of ideological terrorists who "hijack" religion. My concern is that religion can be hijacked in many different ways. Our faith, our religion as Catholics, can be hijacked; and the hijacker, most frequently, is ideology that has given up on searching faith. Let's not allow our faith to be hijacked by ideological terrorists of any stripe.

Michelle Beardon, in the August 8, 2005, *Tampa Tribune,* wrote on the phenomenon of spiritual seekers, people who are looking for spiritual connection and dynamics in their lives, but not necessarily through the traditional institutional organized churches. Seekers might be helped and fed by a church, but they also might find spiritual nourishment via the Internet or take-home materials that they work on in leisure moments.

Beardon writes about churches that are successful, at least in terms of attracting numbers, having been influenced by the training and modeling of the Willow Creek Association. The Willow Creek Association currently has about ten thousand churches around the world networked in its outreaching, evangelizing style. The article demonstrates that Willow Creek has learned to do inculturation well, namely, to take the gospel and use contemporary, popular culture to share it in relevant, life-changing ways.

The title of Beardon's article is "Converting Churches." She talks about how the Willow Creek Association is teaching churches how to change themselves to be more effective in reaching out and evangelizing.

The August 11, 2005, cover story in *USA Today* was on the rapid decline of mainline Christian churches, including Catholicism, in Western Europe, Australia, and the United States. Some of the people quoted in the article seem to be trying to escape ideology, at least in Catholicism. One thirty-nine-year-old man in Dublin, Ireland, said, "I don't know anyone my age who's going to church. Fifteen years ago I didn't know anyone my age who wasn't going to church. I am a spiritual person. I believe in God. I pray to God daily. When I pray it changes me, but I don't need an institution for my spirituality." While I would challenge this young man on the communal nature of faith, I also hear a real disdain for the ideology that comes from hierarchy and clergy.

I challenged myself recently to do a diagnosis of church leadership from the perspective of personality. If some church leaders were sitting across from me in the counseling office, how would I evaluate them? What thoughts would be running through my head in terms of diagnosis?

I sense in many current leaders a paranoid dimension to their leadership. There is mistrust and suspicion toward clergy and laity striving to work with them. I also sense antisocial dynamics. Among many there is a real insensitivity to relationships. One priest said of his archbishop, "He hates his priests; at least that is how it appears, based on his speech and action with us."

Among many leaders I sense a real narcissistic streak. Narcissism, self-centeredness, a grandiose sense of self-importance, runs through the hierarchical and clerical culture.

A seminary system that takes men away from reality and trains them to think that they are ontologically different from others is a breeding ground for narcissism. Priests come out of the seminary not as servant leaders, but as people who see themselves as "different from" and "special."

I sense also in leadership real obsessive-compulsive tendencies. Leaders are preoccupied with details, rules, lists, order, and organization. Within this tendency there is inflexibility, rigidity, stubbornness, and an inability or unwillingness to discard realities that are no longer effective or productive.

In this ecclesial situation it is vital that we get to a practice of the contemplative conversations that Cozzens calls us to. There must be an urgency to reclaim our spiritual authority in the church, and, as both Cozzens and Stephen Covey exhort us, to discover and speak our *voice*. We must do this with fidelity and loyalty to the church and love for the Body of Christ, the church. We must do this with all the good skills of communication and collaboration, but also confidence that the Holy Spirit is working in us, as well as in the bishops, the cardinals, and the pope.

I have been in active ministry since 1972, and in all these years I have never sensed a more somber, concerned mood among church workers than I do now. Some say that what is needed are more churches like Rochester's Spiritus Christi Church, an independent Catholic Church that has broken away from its diocese. That parish is a very successful model, with many people and a healthy sense of financial and ministerial stewardship. I personally do not believe that

that is the direction that most of us should go. I think we should stay invested and involved in creative dialogue on all strata of church life.

I believe that the bishops fear a schism coming in the American Catholic Church. Paradoxically, if they screen people out with their ideology, it is they, more than the rest of us, who would create the schism. All who are marginalized, rejected, judged, and criticized may have to get together for support.

When Luther put his Ninety-Five Theses on the door of the castle church in Wittenberg, I do not believe that he intended to be a heretic. He was rendered a heretic, although all he wanted to do was engage in healthy dialogue about concerns he had regarding church discipline.

Luther was excommunicated for his concerns. The Reformation resulted. The Counter-Reformation in the Catholic Church issued a message that we hear a great deal today: There will be no discussion. This is the way it is. If you do not like it, get out, or we will remove you.

In a challenging book entitled *Simple Truths: On Values, Civility, and Our Common Good,* Rev. Stephen Bauman, pastor of Christ Church in New York City, reflects on the toxic busyness of contemporary Americans. He says there are only a few things that people really need. We need good relationships. We need meaningful conversations. We need to experience the mystery of God. He laments that so much organized religion either obsesses over irrelevant minutia or has entered into collusion with a dominant American political party. Such distortions are examples of what he calls "religion at its worst."

As mission driven parishes and congregations, let's strive for healthy communal relationships, for good learning and conversations with each other. Let's strive to experience and touch the Holy One, as revealed by Jesus Christ.

Transition

In offering Holy Family as an example of a mission driven parish, I am trying to convey to the reader, through a real-life experience, that being mission driven is certainly possible, but it demands planning, setting goals and objectives, and a constant tweaking and massaging of structures to insure that the mission is indeed pursued.

As of this writing in the summer of 2006, I have one year left in a twelve-year term. The cardinal and the Priests' Placement Board have granted me an additional two years to complete a capital campaign and the construction of our new building, the Holy Family Center for Children, Youth, and Families.

If my health holds out, I have three years remaining here. Nonetheless, the parish has begun thinking about pastor transition. For over a year, a Succession Planning Ministering Community has been examining the possibility of having to replace me in one to three years, but has also been discussing a succession plan for any staff member who may move on.

In addition to meeting with the rather large ministry staff, which includes directors, associate directors, and coordinators, as well as the administrative and maintenance staffs, on a regular basis, I have created several new levels of authority. The executive team meets once a month for about an hour and a half over lunch. The executive team consists of the two pastoral associates, the director of finance, the director of operations/parish management, and me. This executive team is an overseer group that discusses both the status quo and the direction of the parish. We also discuss staff management and care, how best to serve the staff as the staff seeks to serve the parish. Quite often these meetings are just open discussions about concerns that each of us has.

A director of operations has been part of the staff for many years. I have asked this staff person, however, to take on other responsibilities in addition to the practical tasks assigned to this position. I have asked this person to be the consultant and resource person for the parish as a system. I have asked this staff person to try to grow in the skills of organizational behavior. We are constantly tweaking our structure, but after fourteen years of essentially the same structure, I have asked the director of operations to critically assess whether our seasoned structure is effectively at the service of the mission. The operations division and its director essentially facilitate the practicalities of all the other ministries and Leadership Communities. It is my hope that the operations director will be the guarantor that the parish has a system, and parish structures are continually being assessed, evaluated, and reshaped for the mission.

I have also asked one of our pastoral associates, who is also the director of Family F.A.I.T.H. and Life, Dawn Mayer, to become the director of pastoral ministry. In this role, she will share pastoring the staff with me. I have asked her to become more acquainted with every division of ministry and the work of each ministry staff member. I have asked her to meet with ministry staff on a regular basis, as I will continue to do, so that each of them might get more pastoral attention and direction in achieving the goals and objectives of their given ministries. I believe that the staff needs more shepherding and care than I can give, and so, in effect, I am trying to share my role of pastoring with the director of pastoral ministry.

Should the day arrive and there is no resident priest, it is my hope that with this structure the parish would effectively be managed under the leadership of these two directors who indeed have the responsibility for the well-being of the entire parish. In this model, pastors could come and go, sacramental ministers and priests could come and go, but the direction of the parish would always remain intact.

HOLY FAMILY PARISH STAFF AND GOVERNANCE

Pastor

Director of Pastoral Ministry

Director of Operations/ Parish Management

Executive Team

Pastor, Director of Worship, Director of Pastoral Ministry, Director of Finance, Director of Operations/Parish Management

Pastoral Associates

Sacramental Ministers & Ministers of Formation

Sacramental Ministers

Pastoral Council

Finance Committee

Adult Formation
Director & Associates

Pastoral Care
Director & Associates

Family F.A.I.T.H. & Life
Director & Associates

Worship
Director & Associates

Youth
Director & Associates

Evangelical Outreach
Director & Associates

Service, Justice & Peace
Director & Associates

Operations
Director & Associates

Key:
Solid line: reporting structure
Dotted line: lay representatives to Pastoral Council

New Image of Parish (Revised)

Holy Family Parish
Twentieth Anniversary Pastoral Plan
2005–2010

I. Introduction

Our Vision

Holy Family Parish is a Catholic Christian Community where all are welcome. By virtue of our baptism we are sent to use our God-given gifts in service to God and others. We are called to evangelize and to witness to God's love and mercy, to bring forgiveness and healing in a broken world, and to help people discern Christ's call to discipleship.

Our Mission

Holy Family Parish exists to help with the emergence of the Reign of God by living the teachings of Jesus Christ. We continue the work of Jesus Christ, inviting all to understand his message of new life in the world. We strive to live the Reign of God. We share our faith in the domestic church of home, in small Christian communities, in our neighborhoods, and in the workplace.

Our Principles and Heart Values

1. **Communication** of Jesus Christ and our faith community to the world around us.

2. **Evangelization** of all people toward conversion and life in God's Reign.

3. The **priesthood of the faithful** and **servant leadership** flowing from baptism, with empowerment through training and formation for ministry.

4. **Stewardship** of time, treasure, and gifts of the Holy Spirit.

5. Responsibility of all for **mercy, justice, and peace.**

6. **Small groups** and **basic Christian communities** as paradigmatic for our parish life.

7. The **domestic church** of home as the basic cell of church.

8. **Healing** a broken Church and world through ministry, dialogue, prayer, forgiveness, and the celebration of the sacraments.

9. A community of lifelong **learners** committed to religious education from childhood through adulthood.

10. Embracing the **diversity** of all God's people.

The Context in Which We Minister

DEMOGRAPHIC. Six surrounding communities, Barrington, Hoffman Estates, Inverness, Palatine, Schaumburg and South Barrington, comprise 92 percent of parish membership. Our church is situated in the Village of Inverness, which is primarily a residential community that accounts for approximately 4 percent of the Holy Family membership.

Many parishioners have attended Catholic elementary and secondary schools. Fewer have university degrees from Catholic institutions.

Transient members, those moving in five or fewer years, can be easily overlooked. Their needs, especially to be involved on a time-bound basis, can be addressed by our welcoming and inviting initiatives.

While available demographic data is limited, we know that many Holy Family parishioners are mature, well educated, and technical/management oriented. Many contribute freely of their time, treasure, and talent and are models of sacrificial giving. However, giving and its purposes must make sense to a large, thoughtfully critical section of the parish. Capital campaigns, endowment funds, and legacy projects will benefit from well-developed and implemented fund-raising plans. An important aspect of any such plan must be thoughtful communication and comprehensive explanations to the entire parish community.

Public awareness of the sexual abuse scandal will be problematic for decades as reflected in the John Jay Study. Additionally, the recent liturgical reforms have challenged the parish to incorporate practices that have not been a part of this parish's history.

ECONOMIC AND FINANCIAL. Demand for Holy Family Parish support programs appears to increase during a weakened/recovering economy. Even in these difficult times our income is relatively stable. The loss of employment, underemployment, career dislocation, and relocations continue to stress parishioners' lives.

Holy Family parishioners have been generous in their financial support. Holy Family budgets more than $2,000,000 income each year. During winter 2004, weekly collections averaged $43,000. Recent trends have shown that Holy Family experiences little income decline following an economic downturn. There is some indication, however, that church-related crises do impact parishioner support, even if only temporarily. The national parishioner household tithing average is $824 per year. If Holy Family were able to achieve this average it would result in $3,000,000 annually.

While support has been generous, this data suggests the possibility of asking for even greater sacrificial giving. We strive to be a tithing parish, giving 10 percent of all that we receive in offerings to mercy and justice needs. We hope that parishioners similarly grow in a personal tithing pattern.

How We Seek to Live Our Values

Holy Family Parish strives to live out its mission and values. Worship at Holy Family seeks to proclaim the good news of the gospel. We seek to be a sign of God's forgiveness and mercy while we invite all deeper into the mystery of God's love and presence in the world. We seek to embrace the vision of Vatican II. We are challenged to always remain open and inviting in our decision making. We use the discernment model to reach consensus in our parish governance.

Parish leadership has embraced the gifts of our communities, which has allowed our ministries to grow. Holy Family Parish was founded on welcoming, inviting, and nurturing principles. After twenty years it is possible that parishioner and staff member sensitivity to welcoming, invitation, and nurturing can become dull. Internal changes that facilitated parish growth and governance can supplant or diffuse core values. An essential element of this plan is to reinvigorate welcoming, inviting, and nurturing, which are hallmarks of our parish.

We are blessed with a gifted pastor, exceptional sacramental and formation ministers, staff, and lay leadership. Liturgical excellence is derived from the presence of the Holy Spirit, consistent vibrant theology, relevant and uplifting homilies and music, and the stewardship of gifted parishioners. Willingness of the parish leadership to listen and collaborate with parishioner concerns continues to be invaluable. Striving for excellence in our liturgies for future years is a major element of this plan.

Our Challenge

Holy Family Parish has chosen an ambitious mission, value and principle set. To achieve these goals, the parish must continue to develop a cadre of qualified lay leaders and ministers. The parish must also generate the necessary financial support to maintain and ensure our mission. Parish consensus, especially on mission and values, is needed on the widest possible basis. During the founding years, the parish was knit by common needs and aspirations. Today, we have become much larger and more diverse. Common needs and aspirations are sometimes found more in Ministering Communities than parish-wide.

In this twentieth anniversary document, two challenges are identified as paramount: actualizing our heart values, and reinforcing leadership and leadership practices. Both are addressed through thoughtful selection of the larger parish goals and development of unique ministry goals and objectives. This will benefit all parishioners as well as those serving in individual ministries.

In Jesus' name and through his example, we strive to build future church at Holy Family by becoming a more welcoming, inviting, and nurturing community.

Parish Needs

Calls for leadership and ministry training have been consistent and fairly broad-based. Presently, identification and development of leadership ability is found in leadership selection and ministry mentoring. Potential exists for leadership training to be added to CALLED or other adult education programs. Some training requirements are common to many ministries and others are specific to individuals. Currently, Holy Family lacks an inventory of training and formation needs and a coordinated vehicle for developing them.

We need to improve and strengthen our recruitment of potential leaders into all of our ministries in order to provide continuity and succession.

Any perceived need for cultural change must be viewed as a need for renewal and commitment to parish values. The ministries and structures to affect a renewal of our welcoming, inviting, and nurturing qualities are in-place. The process generating this plan has provided a substantive number of parishioner ideas and suggestions for goals.

While the need for youth and young adult programs is being addressed by new staff and renewed emphasis on evangelization, this part of parish life shares prominence in our pastor's vision. Outreach to these parishioners is highlighted for attention by all ministries.

II. Parish Goals and Objectives

Goal 1: Holy Family will deepen its commitment to evangelization as its central mission.

Objective 1. The eight Leadership Communities and all ministries will continue to study, talk about, and live out the convergence model of evangelization; that is, all the efforts of the parish converge on one mission — to evangelize.

Objective 2. The eight Leadership Communities and all Ministering Communities will have as an objective to study, talk about, and live the convergence model. All parish ministries will be trained on how they can help parishioners with the journey of conversion.

Objective 3. All ministries and ministers will continue to pray, study, and grow in the understanding of what Jesus meant by the Reign of God.

Objective 4. Mark 1:15 (This is the time of fulfillment. The Kingdom of God is at hand. Repent, and believe in the Gospel) and Luke 4:43 (Jesus said, "I must proclaim the Good News. It was for this reason I was sent.") will become underpinning scriptural passages for the work of the parish.

Objective 5. Holy Family will invite all newcomers, as well as people in sacramental preparation years, to a new Mini-Retreat on what it means to be a responsible member of Holy Family Parish.

Objective 6. We will evaluate the effectiveness of the current practice of welcoming newcomers at the greeting part of the Mass along with the newcomer cards and the procedures for follow-up. A standard script for welcoming will be prepared for presiders.

Objective 7. A new Welcoming Ministry will be begun as part of Evangelical Outreach. An associate director will be appointed to lead this ministry. The role of this person will be to develop a concierge-like ministry for the church narthex, where trained volunteers will be placed every weekday evening and after all liturgies on the weekends. The role of the welcoming minister will be to help all parishioners, but especially newcomers, to find their way, both through the physical complex, and Holy Family's many ministerial offerings.

Objective 8. The new Welcoming Ministry will host a quarterly breakfast or brunch, in cooperation with the Knights' Café, to check on the spiritual journey of newcomers.

Objective 9. At welcoming sessions, newcomers will be given Gifted materials to begin the process of discerning gifts for stewardship of time and giftedness.

Objective 10. All newcomers will be educated at the Sunday welcoming session on responsible financial stewardship.

Objective 11. All newcomers will be welcomed into Small Christian Communities, or Bible Study, at the Sunday welcoming gathering.

Objective 12. All newcomers will be given copies of the parish mission statement, vision statement, and heart values as well as an overview of the parish governance structure to better understand what is involved in responsible membership.

Objective 13. Public relations/marketing will be a ministry that is intensified and supported.

Objective 14. Holy Family's communications ministries will add a tone of outreach to all radio, TV, and Internet offerings.

Objective 15. Our Internet ministry will be expanded with improvements on our website, and expansion of *The Stream,* or Internet radio.

Communications will explore more expansive syndication of our offerings on radio and the possibilities of use of satellite radio.

Objective 16. All in parish leadership will engage in an ongoing conversation and study as to how to engage and evangelize secularity.

Goal 2: Holy Family will deepen and develop its efforts at the re-evangelization of active Catholics.

Objective 1. Community on Wednesday will be offered multiple times during the year to provide all involved in parish ministry and parish life with a healthy experience of community and re-evangelization.

Objective 2. Holy Family's new Welcoming Ministry will do follow-up work with all who have celebrated sacraments in the last three to five years.

Objective 3. Holy Family will sharpen its use of the steps of the RCIA as a way to evangelize all who are seeking sacraments.

Objective 4. Holy Family will continue and improve its efforts at family-based religious education.

Objective 5. Holy Family will quantitatively multiply Small Christian Communities by at least 25 percent each year by three deliberate and intentional sign-up opportunities to be in Small Christian Communities, or Bible Study.

Objective 6. Family F.A.I.T.H. will continue to move its processes toward the paradigm of clusters of families doing religious education together.

Objective 7. Adult Faith Formation will be more intentional in discerning the adult needs of the faith community. Adult learning opportunities will be offered for those needs, which in a parallel way can help parishioners grow in faith.

Objective 8. A Parish Mission Ministering Community will be established to annually offer a quality religious experience through a parish mission.

Objective 9. Parish retreats will be improved. Current models include Kingdom, Christ Renews His Parish, and Marriage Encounter. A new retreat will be developed around the themes of contemplation and social justice. The director of Adult Faith Formation is responsible for improving parish retreats.

Objective 10. Use of the Medard Laz Wisdom Center for parish retreats will be studied. Changes will be made so that retreats offered on the parish site will be comfortable and meaningful.

Objective 11. The Mini-Retreat model benchmarked from other parishes will be established in the winter of 2005.

Objective 12. All adult learning experiences will be either audiotaped or videotaped for purchase, or lending, so that people can use these materials in their own private time.

Objective 13. A parish retreat will be put on tape to be experienced either alone or in a small group in people's homes.

Objective 14. CALLED will continue to be developed for the training of parish leaders.

Objective 15. All eight divisions of parish life will offer regular ministry training/formation experiences for both experienced and new ministers. Adult Faith Formation will publish a synthesis of all ministry offerings at least twice a year.

Objective 16. The School of Ministry will be improved. It will strengthen our relationship with universities, so that BA and MA level course offerings may be experienced on the campus of Holy Family. In addition to the Catholic Theological Union, Dominican University, and Loyola University Pastoral Ministry Institute in New Orleans, we will develop a relationship with the Institute of Pastoral Studies at Loyola University Chicago. Hopefully this relationship will work toward a LIMEX model of graduate work at our parish. LIMEX is an extension program of the Loyola Institute for Ministry at Loyola University in New Orleans.

Objective 17. Holy Family staff and leadership will continue efforts at improving our Gifted process to help parishioners in the process of discernment of gifts of time, treasure, and spiritual charisms.

Objective 18. Holy Family will continue to foster its Neighborhood Ministry program in an effort to cast an evangelical relational net over the geographical territory of the parish. In the next two years, at least fifty neighborhood ministers will be added each year.

Goal 3: Holy Family will improve its efforts at the evangelization of inactive, alienated, or hurting members.

Objective 1. The parish's current Landings program will be enhanced through improved marketing and public relations.

Objective 2. Neighborhood ministers will be given special training in how to reach out to and minister to inactive members.

Objective 3. The parish's new Welcoming follow-up ministry for those involved in sacramental catechesis will be given special training in ministering to inactive members.

Objective 4. The Reconciling Parish, a process for those deeply hurt or alienated from the church, will be begun in 2004-2005.

Objective 5. Beginning in the fall of 2004, the parish will revitalize its ministry to the divorced with a new educational effort, Rising from Divorce. The children and families of those touched by divorce will be included in this new model.

Objective 6. Beginning in the fall of 2004, parish leadership will ask the question "Whom are we no longer seeing?" The parish will then reach out to these people in pursuit of causality and in an attempt to reconcile where necessary and possible.

Objective 7. Pastoral Care will deepen and expand its efforts at helping ministries addressing the psychological, relational, and spiritual woundedness of contemporary people. Special attention will be given to those suffering loss, grief, anxiety, and depression. This will be done in conjunction with the new Center for Inner Peace, Hope, Forgiveness, and Reconciliation.

Objective 8. The parish will improve marketing and public relations efforts oriented toward inactive Catholics. This will be done through print, cable access, Internet, and radio spots.

Objective 9. The parish will use the parish's regular and expanded reconciliation celebrations to welcome home those who have been far from the church.

Goal 4: Holy Family will become more committed to reach out to the unchurched.

Objective 1. Through better marketing and public relations efforts in print, audio, video, and Internet efforts, the parish will better reach out to the unchurched.

Objective 2. Footsteps in Faith, our RCIA process, will increase quantitatively the number of unchurched invited into the process by 25 percent each year in the next five years.

Objective 3. Holy Family's Young Adult ministry will expand by 25 percent in attendance at events each year in the next five years.

Objective 4. Holy Family's Young Adult ministry will develop connections with our parishioners at commuter colleges and also at other universities.

Objective 5. Holy Family will continue to offer needs-based adult learning like The First Five Years (of Marriage) to connect with people on the level of felt need or struggle.

Objective 6. Year-long inquiry, or pre-evangelization, will continue and be deepened and improved for those interested in the RCIA process.

Objective 7. Holy Family will continue its ministry to and celebration of single life.

Goal 5: Holy Family will dramatically improve its efforts to evangelize youth in the next two to five years.

Objective 1. By the fall of 2005, Holy Family will articulate a five-year plan for the improvement of youth ministry and youth evangelization.

Objective 2. Holy Family will continue to build on its RCIA-like process of T.O.R.C.H., Ignite, F.L.A.M.E., Celebrating the Spirit, peer ministry, and retreat ministries.

Objective 3. Holy Family will expand F.L.A.M.E. small groups, helping them to extend into the junior and senior years.

Objective 4. Holy Family will continue to improve its effort at touching older teens, especially with the development of the Kairos model of retreat, and junior/senior F.L.A.M.E. groups.

Objective 5. Holy Family will develop a School of Ministry for teens, inviting them into the ministry for which they are developmentally capable.

Objective 6. Holy Family will be sensitive to ministering to those already confirmed in elementary school grades by offering deliberate and intentional ministries to these young parishioners.

Objective 7. The director of Youth Ministries and staff will offer regular training and formation processes for parents and volunteer ministers who are working with teens.

Objective 8. A parent organization to serve as advocates for youth ministry will be developed within the next two years.

Objective 9. The various pieces of youth ministry will be brought into a more cooperative and synthetic process, operating as if each piece flows into the next.

Objective 10. Holy Family youth ministry and evangelization will continue to develop out of and improve our commitment to two principles: organic growth and maximum influence. Organic growth means that we will continue to develop a core group of teen leaders who will minister to a circle of regularly practicing teens in small groups; and in turn, these active teens will deliberately and intentionally reach out to a next circle of adolescents who are functionally unchurched, inviting them into the various activities and ministries of the parish.

Objective 11. Youth Ministry will explore how to improve our social offerings for teens to help them discover the parish as a "home" for young people.

Objective 12. Holy Family youth ministry will become more aware of those activities that are important to teens and try to have a presence at such meetings and events.

Objective 13. Holy Family, on a regular basis, will hold large group youth rallies to offer inspiring experiential large group evangelization.

Objective 14. Holy Family will continue to celebrate a 5:00 p.m. Sunday Mass, planned and ministered by high-school youth.

Goal 6: Holy Family will continue to evangelize the active, the inactive, the unchurched, and all age demographic groups by continuing to develop its progressive evangelical style of worship.

Objective 1. Music Ministry will continue in an evangelical/eclectic fashion.

Objective 2. Presiders will be engaged based upon the quality of their spirituality and on their reputation of being excellent preachers and presiders. All liturgical ministers will converge to offer enthusiastic worship.

Objective 3. There will be a fostering of the arts to complement liturgy. This will include plays, concerts, musicals, and other artistic forms.

Objective 4. Those with the gift of preaching will be encouraged to speak God's Word.

Objective 5. Preachers will deliver messages containing a livable spirituality with relevance for all: multi-generational groups, families, singles, divorced and young adults. Teaching opportunities in preaching will be offered.

Objective 6. The Worship Space will be remodeled to better accommodate the use of AV technology, to engage the congregation in full participation including handicap access. The space will be aesthetically improved.

Goal 7: Holy Family will continue to evangelize the domestic church of family.

Objective 1. Holy Family will engage in efforts to improve Family F.A.I.T.H., toward the vision of Clusters of Families/Small Christian Community model.

Objective 2. Continued and improved efforts will be made in the area of marriage preparation and marriage enrichment.

Objective 3. Regular offerings on parenting education will be continued and improved. Common Sense Parenting will continue to be offered.

Objective 4. Family F.A.I.T.H. will have a cooperative relationship with Holy Family Catholic Academy, especially in the area of texts and praxis for catechesis and sacramental preparation.

Objective 5. Holy Family Catholic Academy will be grown to evangelize families, in cooperation with parochial schools in the area, and with the archdiocesan school system.

Objective 6. As Family F.A.I.T.H., Holy Family Catholic Academy, Youth Ministry, and Adult Faith Formation and other areas of parish life continue to grow, the need for additional space will be researched and discerned. Needed fund-raising will be done to accomplish this objective.

Objective 7. Holy Family will significantly move family-based religious education to a Sabbath-weekend model. These offerings will be connected with one of our weekend liturgies, will have age-appropriate worship and catechesis for children, teens, and adults in parallel offerings. Media, drama, and music will present livable messages that inculturate the gospel.

Objective 8. Holy Family pastoral staff and parish families will enter into a covenant of mutual expectations to better accomplish the evangelization of its children, teens, and adults.

Objective 9. In addition to the covenant, staff and parents will continue to develop in our young people, the 40 developmental assets articulated by the Search Institute.

Goal 8: Holy Family will better use the media to evangelize.

Objective 1. Holy Family marketing and public relations ministry will expand.

Objective 2. Holy Family will expand our networks for our radio and TV offerings.

Objective 3. Holy Family will develop a cable access program oriented toward teens.

Objective 4. Holy Family will place our Mass on a UHF station with a strong signal.

Objective 5. Holy Family will develop various forms of Internet ministry including *The Stream,* or Internet radio.

Objective 6. Holy Family will develop an Internet tree of communication, whereby we can communicate with all, or most, parishioners via e-mail.

Objective 7. Holy Family will develop a Holy Family chat room where people can connect with the parish for education and information.

Objective 8. Holy Family will explore the many ways to use print, e.g., newspapers and magazines, to evangelize.

Objective 9. Holy Family will begin anew our *Connections* newsletter to be placed in local papers at least twice a year. The newsletter ought to have a seasonal Advent/Christmas, Spring /Easter/Summer focus.

Goal 9: Holy Family will deepen its commitment to become a stewardship parish.

Objective 1. We will continue to educate the parish about the importance of holistic stewardship at least twice a year at weekend liturgies. We will provide a regular accounting of how parish resources have been used.

Objective 2. Ten percent of all that we collect will be dedicated to mercy and justice.

Objective 3. A vision of holistic stewardship will become one of the educational components of our regular offerings at newcomers welcoming sessions.

Objective 4. Parishioners will be encouraged to imitate the parish's practice of giving 10 percent of income to mercy and justice needs.

Goal 10: Holy Family will grow in its understanding of and involvement in the work of mercy and justice.

Objective 1. The Service, Justice and Peace Community will educate the parish regularly on the qualities of social teaching, responsible citizenship and discipleship. This education will be emphasized prior to state and national elections.

Objective 2. The Service, Justice and Peace Community will aid each Leadership Community in articulating a mercy/justice investment in which the Leadership Community will be involved.

Objective 3. The Service, Justice and Peace Community will provide ongoing education to individuals, Ministering Communities, Small Christian Communities, Bible Study groups, and families on steps for moving toward mercy and justice involvement. The Michael Cowan model, given to the parish some years ago, will be the preferred discernment process for this.

Objective 4. The leaders in the Service, Justice and Peace Community will help the parish to understand that the call to discipleship involves commutative, distributive, and social justice for all people.

Objective 5. The Service, Justice and Peace Community will continue to discern the need for various mercy/justice ministries.

Objective 6. The Service, Justice and Peace Community will pilot a thirty-week education justice process entitled "Just Faith" beginning in the fall of 2005.

Goal II: Holy Family Parish will begin to explore ways to evangelize in cooperation with other Christian church and faith communities.

Objective 1. A new ecumenism ministry will be begun to explore communication and work with other faith expressions.

Objective 2. Special prayer services of an ecumenical nature will be offered in a cooperative way with other denominations at Thanksgiving and Pentecost time.

Objective 3. Holy Family will invite churches of all denominations to its spring 2005 Purpose Driven Church conference.

Objective 4. Holy Family will explore the revival of the old "network" concept, an attempt to network Catholic and other congregations in an alliance toward excellence in ministry and evangelization. This alliance/network will be an ongoing source of support and education.

III. Critical Issues

Some action plans have already been developed to address critical parish issues. Our pastor has reformed the ministry organization to better serve our evangelizing mission, to balance workloads, and to renew small Christian communities and neighborhoods. Our new organization is declared in time for preparation of this plan and will be in full effect for 2004–2005.

Two critical issues will demand our attention through the early years of this plan — space and training. We are awaiting diocesan recommendations for Catholic school planning in Vicariate 1. The results will influence how the parish addresses the needs of Youth Ministry and Family F.A.I.T.H., as well as Holy Family Catholic Academy. Renovations to the worship space, parish ministry space needs, as well as Holy Family Catholic Academy needs, must be resolved early in the planning period. Leadership and ministry training needs must be assessed and plans developed to meet these needs within parish resources.

IV. Ministry Goals

Each individual Ministering Community will be asked to present goals to their Leadership Communities which reflect the goals and objectives contained in this document.

V. Recommendations

Further development of demographics and environmental data will help the parish reach its giving potential. It is recommended that future surveys, while continuing to define the pastoral topics, address parish financial attitudes and opportunities in greater detail.

As the parish continues to move along its faith cycle, a broad-based review of vision, mission, and values will be needed every three years to maintain consensus. It is recommended that this review be conducted before the planning cycle begins and be performed by a broadly selected group of parishioners, staff, and leadership.

Every planning committee has emphasized the need for clear and unambiguous internal communication. Holy Family has greatly extended the reach of its internal parish communications during recent years. It is recommended that some methods be considered to evaluate the effectiveness of the communication.

The parish must continue the praxis of integrated collaboration for processes that cross areas of responsibility, e.g., Pastoral Council, Leadership, Staff, Finance, Pastor, and Membership.

All ministries and parishioners are challenged to become intentional, proactive evangelizers, witnessing to the Reign of God in the home, in the workplace, and in the neighborhood.

Holy Family will strive to be a beacon of hope in the midst of the chaos and confusion of this time by always keeping our eyes fixed on Jesus and striving in many ways to be an evangelizing parish.